THE POWER OF
Pause

D1016418

TERRY HERSHEY

THE POWER OF
Pause

Becoming More
by Doing Less

LOYOLA PRESS.
A JESUIT MINISTRY
Chicago

LOYOLA PRESS.
A JESUIT MINISTRY

3441 N. Ashland Avenue
Chicago, Illinois 60657
(800) 621-1008
www.loyolapress.com

© 2009 Terry Hershey
All rights reserved

Cover image © Roine Magnusson/Getty Images
Cover design by Judine O'Shea
Interior design by Kathryn Seckman Kirsh and Joan Bledig

Library of Congress Cataloging-in-Publication Data
Hershey, Terry.
 The power of pause : becoming more by doing less / Terry Hershey.
  p. cm.
 ISBN-13: 978-0-8294-2862-9
 ISBN-10: 0-8294-2862-3
 1. Simplicity—Religious aspects—Christianity. 2. Time management—
Religious aspects—Christianity. I. Title.
 BV4647.S48H47 2009
 248.4—dc22

First paperback printing: November 2010
ISBN-13: 978-0-8294-3546-7
ISBN-10: 0-8294-3546-8

Printed in the United States of America
10 11 12 13 14 15 16 Versa 10 9 8 7 6 5 4 3 2 1

To Zach

~~~~~~~~~~~~~~~~

CONTENTS

Part Six: Late Summer

Part Seven: Early Autumn

Part Eight: Late Autumn

A Word from Terry

*Living artfully with time might only require something
as simple as pausing.*

—THOMAS MOORE, *CARE OF THE SOUL*

We live in a world that urges us to admire and pursue
whatever is faster, whatever is newer, and whatever is
bigger—the underlying idea being that we should be living a
different life, not the one we're living now.

We worship at the altar of the superlative. This is no surprise
given the model by which we quantify success. Since we crave
speed and we see productivity as our objective, these things
become our standards for measuring how well we're doing.

"What did you accomplish today?"

"Are you kidding?" is our response, "I'm important.
Look—no white spaces on my calendar." There are times when
I feel rewarded for being so busy. *Sometimes,* I tell myself, *a little
exhaustion is worth a pat on the back.*

But here's the disquieting truth: a life based upon speed
and productivity demands a high price. I know what it is like
to sacrifice a marriage because I was very busy, working hard
for Jesus. As a young clergyman, I had a career in church work

that was successful and prominent. I polished the image of my importance, and I received public accolades. Unfortunately, in my busyness I said no to the people most important to me. And I lived a divided life, not a whole life and certainly not a holy one. I don't want to live that way anymore.

It takes some courage, but we have to ask some probing questions.

Have you ever felt overwhelmed, only to add more to your to-do list?

Have you ever felt rushed, wishing for a wand that would enable you to slow down time?

Have you ever wished for an extra day in your week?

Have you ever been in a conversation when it hits you, *I'm not really here?*

Has your plate of obligations ever been so full that you felt frozen, unable to move?

Have you ever been rewarded for working while exhausted?

Have you ever felt pulled in so many directions that you did not feel at home in your own skin?

Have you ever agreed to a commitment when you knew that the only healthy answer was no?

Have you ever tried to pray, only to find your mind swimming with yesterday's worries?

Have you ever answered the question, "How are you?" with any one of these expressions, "My life is . . . so hectic, too full, very complicated, jam-packed, behind and can't catch up—if only I had time to answer your question"?

Have you ever wanted to pause long enough to see the handprint of God in the clouds, or in the face of a stranger, or in the irritation of the chaotic, or in the touch of friend, or in the ordinary events of the day?

If so, *The Power of Pause* is for you. It extends the invitation to do less, and become more.

Will this book change your life? If you are willing to practice the power of pause, the answer is assuredly, yes.

What We're Made For

You must have a place to which you can go in your heart, your mind, or your house, almost every day, where you do not owe anyone and where no one owes you—a place that simply allows for the blossoming of something new and promising.

JOSEPH CAMPBELL, *THE POWER OF MYTH*

We are wired to be present. We are built to honor the senses. We are created to be attentive, or literally just to *be*. But somewhere along the way, life chokes the music and poetry out of us. *The Power of Pause* is good for what ails us. It is based on the principle of Sabbath. *Sabbath* means to cease and to rest. Sabbath is a cornerstone of the Jewish faith and is affirmed by the Christian faith. In fact, the practice of Sabbath resonates with persons of every faith and religious tradition—and even those with no tradition at all. That's because most traditions recognize that we have not only a *doing* space but a *being* space. In that doing space we work, achieve, accomplish, and produce. But in the being space are prayer, touch, rest, wonderment, and, if we are lucky, unrepentant napping.

"The power of pause. I like it," a man told me after a workshop. "So what do I do?"

Our techno-thinking kicks in. What are the five steps to pausing? How do we "do" Sabbath? What is the technique? We see an imbalanced life as requiring a technological fix. As a result, we try to alleviate or correct our situation by using the very same tools or resources or thinking that got us into the pickle in the first place. Can you believe that in a bookstore I found a book titled *One-Minute Bedtime Stories*? It is for parents who don't have enough time.

The Power of Pause is not only about what we do but also about what we *don't* do. Is it possible that I can become a better me, not by addition, but by subtraction?

There are two kinds of pause. One is passive: I stop, I let go, I'm still, and I breathe out.

The other pause is active: I am attentive, I'm conscious in this moment, I take responsibility for the life I have right now, and I breathe in.

Why call this the *power* of pause? Because there is power in our awareness that our choices do in fact make a difference. The Power of Pause is the . . .

Power to pay attention

In the Jewish understanding of Shabbat—the day of pausing, or day of rest—we are to celebrate *time* rather than *space*. Six days out of the week we live under the tyranny of space or stuff. Shabbat is the day we are tuned into the holiness of time. Tuned into the reality that there are no unsacred moments. We can know that every moment is, in fact, touched by the presence and reality of God.

Power to be centered

If you've seen photos of Gandhi, there will inevitably be one of him sitting at his spinning wheel. Gandhi's spinning wheel was his center of gravity. It was the great leveler in his human experience. The spinning wheel was always a reminder to Gandhi of who he was and of what the practical things in life were all about. In engaging in this regular exercise, he resisted all the forces of his public world that tried to distort who he knew himself to be.

Power to say yes to the moment and no to urgency

When I am constrained by urgency, I am making a decision about my identity. I am manipulated by my need to be hurried, to impress, or to stay distracted.

When I give up that need for urgency and say, "No, this can wait," I can do so because I know that I have value apart from the externals in my life. I have the permission just to be, to embrace the sacred present.

Power to listen

A little boy once said to his mother, "Mama, listen to me, but this time with your eyes." Listening is primarily about being present. When we hurry, we develop tunnel vision. We are focused on a destination, so we see only what we want to see and we hear only what we want to hear. Pausing helps us stop and notice things outside the tunnel vision. We see or hear or notice or recognize something as it is, and not as we expected it to be.

Power to see, hear, taste, touch, and smell

> The miracles of the church seem to me to rest not so much on faces or voices or healing power suddenly near to us from afar off, but upon our perceptions being made finer, so that for a moment our eyes can see and our ears can hear what is there about us always.
>
> —*Willa Cather, Death Comes to the Archbishop*

Power to own, to take responsibility for, and to embrace my uniqueness

Each one of us is a unique child of God. When my identity comes from that awareness, I am no longer defined by what I have achieved, or what I consume, or how fast I go, or how busy I am, or how much I earn. I can live *this* life, and not some life yet to be. I can live *from* acceptance, and not *for* acceptance." It is a divine reminder that life is lived from the inside out, from what Thomas Kelly called a "divine center" . . . a place of "power and peace and serenity and integration and confidence."

We need to be careful that we do not become pause consumers, as if we are shopping for an experience, or as if pausing needs to be measured. We don't want to be like the man who told the doctor, "I want to learn how to relax, but I want to relax better and faster than anyone else has ever relaxed before!"

So enter into this day-by-day or week-by-week experience of pausing. Who knows? You just might find a new you—or rediscover the you who has been buried under the clutter and press of the hectic. The you who is more aware, present, energized, real, and authentic. And fully alive.

Using This Book the Way You Need It

There's no best way to use this book. We've arranged it in a way that makes for flexible and variable modes of participation. I'm a gardener, and so I refer quite a lot to gardening and to nature in general. So we placed the chapters in a long cycle of seasons, beginning with early autumn and ending with late summer. We know that there's a difference between early and late, whether it's winter or spring; the early and late parts of the seasons feel different and make us think and sense things differently.

The material in these chapters is all about helping you pause, and that's an interior kind of process. Processes of the soul don't happen all at once but go through phases. So within each physical season we've arranged stories that follow, in a loose way, a fairly common soul cycle.

- Need/Desire
- Stillness/Sanctuary
- Awareness/Astonishment
- Contentment/Embrace
- Choice/Becoming
- Freedom/Celebration

Notice that I said that the stories in each season *loosely* follow this process. There's a lot of overlap; one story might be about awareness but it also might be about choice—there are no hard-and-fast rules here. But if you want or need a story about freedom, please feel *free* to go to that season's last story, which is in the "freedom/celebration" category.

All that to say, we've put stories into seasons because many folks like to follow the physical seasons of the year. And we've categorized stories according to what mood or phase your soul might be in at the time. Choose them and use them as you see fit. This book is for you, to help you pause no matter what mood or season you're in.

〜 **Determine** how much you pause already: visit www.loyolapress.com/powerofpause and click on Book Extras to take The Power of Pause Assessment. Write your score here to help you track your progress: _____

Letting Our Souls Catch Up

By means of a diversion, we can avoid our own company twenty-four hours a day.

—PASCAL, ADAPTED FROM *PENSES*

An American traveler planned a long safari to Africa. He was a compulsive man, loaded down with maps, timetables, and agendas. Men had been engaged from a local tribe to carry the cumbersome load of supplies, luggage, and "essential stuff."

On the first morning, they all woke very early and traveled very fast and went very far. On the second morning, they all woke very early and traveled very fast and went very far. On the third morning, they all woke very early and traveled very fast and went very far. And the American seemed pleased. On the fourth morning, the tribesmen refused to move. They simply sat by a tree. The American became incensed. "This is a waste of valuable time. Can someone tell me what is going on here?"

The translator answered, "They are waiting for their souls to catch up with their bodies."

The sacred necessity of stillness is an invitation to savor the pleasure of slowness and the moments of stillness or even silence, letting them work their magic.

In her book *The Solace of Open Spaces*, Gretel Ehrlich talks about the idea that space can heal, that space—created by silence—represents sanity. Silence can be a fullness rather than a void. It can allow the mind to run through its paces without any need for justification. It can let us recover those parts of the self that have been so scattered, so disparate, throughout the week. To sit still is a spiritual endeavor.

To sit still is to practice Sabbath, which means, literally, to quit.

To stop.
To take a break.
To make uncluttered time.
To waste time with God.

~~~~~~

A Powerful Pause for the Days Ahead

Find a bench to sit on. If you can, buy a new or used bench or chair just for sitting, preferably outside. Practice going to that spot at least once a day just to stop, to quit, to let your soul catch up.

PART ONE

Early Winter

I

Fear and Dancing

To watch us dance is to hear our heart speak.

—HOPI SAYING

In the 1930s when Gillian was a child, her teachers considered her learning disabled, one of those students who didn't pay attention or focus, and who could not sit still. ADHD was not yet a diagnosis, so Gillian was labeled "difficult." And her parents were deeply troubled.

A school counselor arranged a meeting with Gillian and her parents to discuss the options. Through the entire meeting, Gillian sat on her hands, stoic, doing her best to act natural and well behaved. At the end, the counselor asked to see Gillian's parents privately, outside the office. Before he left the room, he turned on his radio. Music filled the office. Outside the office door, the counselor asked Gillian's parents to look back inside at their daughter. No longer seated, Gillian now moved about the room with the music—free, untroubled, and blissful.

"You see," the counselor told the parents, "your daughter isn't sick. She's a dancer."

This story could have gone another way. Gillian could have been labeled and medicated. Problem solved.

Instead, she was given the freedom to live from the inside out. The result? A lifetime of dance on stage and in films, and an extensive career as choreographer for shows such as *Cats* and *The Phantom of the Opera.* Difficult little Gillian became the great Gillian Lynne.

In our hearts, we are all dancers. It is that part of us that responds freely to the music of abundant life. But somewhere along the way, we lose that. And we choose to live guarded and closed. Our fears, or the fears of others, label us, restrict us, and eventually dismiss us and whatever gifts we have to offer.

To dance is to live with arms open, without fear—kind of like four-year-olds. Just ask them: Can you sing? *If we don't know the words, we'll make 'em up.* Can you play music? *A cardboard box and a stick will do.* Can you dance? *Watch this!* Ask an adult: Can you sing? *Only in the shower, and then off-key.* Can you play music? *That was years ago.* Can you dance? *Not without people laughing.*

The music pulsated from a Latin band playing salsa. I was the learner, the beginner on the dance floor, acutely aware of my fears, knowing my left-footedness would make me look goofy. But I watched others and was truly mesmerized; they were lost in the music, their bodies fluid. The woman teaching me said with some regularity, "Quit furrowing. You are furrowing," referring to my brow scrunched in concentration. I was not, in fact, dancing. I was too busy counting steps. I couldn't quite let go. I couldn't quite let myself *just be* a dancer.

I take two lessons from Gillian's story. One: the voice of Grace tells us that we are more than our labels, such as "difficult" or "odd." It's not that we choose to dance so much as we choose to give up being afraid.

We give up being afraid by responding to the love of the Beloved. Gillian's counselor and parents loved her by giving her permission to be who she was. In the stillness of a sacred pause, we can hear the voice of God's love and experience the permission that frees us. Our dance is the interplay with that love, which makes our hearts alive and unafraid.

I'll paraphrase what Robert Capon said in *Between Noon and Three*: Because of fear we live life like ill-taught piano students. So worried over the flub that gets us in Dutch, we don't hear the music, we only play the right notes.

The second lesson: I don't hear this voice of Grace (or invitation to dance) when my life is filled with noise and hurry, when I'm out of breath and out of time, incessantly worried about public opinion.

Which gives me one more good reason to pause and let the music of the sacred summon me.

Inspirations

Dance in Your Blood

Dance, when you're broken open.

Dance, if you've torn the bandage off.

Dance in the middle of the fighting.

Dance in your blood.

Dance, when you're perfectly free.

—RUMI, QUOTED IN *DANCING WITH JOY*

BY ROGER HOUSDEN

~~~~~~~~~~~~~~~~~~~~~~~~~~~~~~~~

A Powerful Pause for the Days Ahead

Put on some music you really like, and listen for a while. Name the things you're afraid of while the music surrounds you. Then move a little to the music and imagine those fears floating away on those beautiful sounds.

2

Two Spaces

*Sabbath time is a revolutionary challenge to the violence
of overwork, because it honors the necessary wisdom of
dormancy. . . . During Sabbath, when we take our
hand from the plow and let the earth care for things,
while we drink, if just briefly, from the fountain of rest
and delight.*

—WAYNE MULLER, *SABBATH*

Every day after school, the son of a well-known rabbi would
enter his house, place his backpack on the dining room
table, leave the house through the back door, and head into the
woods behind the house.

At first, the rabbi gave little thought to his son's ritual. But it
continued for days, and then for weeks. Every day, out into the
woods for almost a half hour. The rabbi grew concerned.

"My son," he said one day. "I notice that every day you leave
our home to spend time in the woods. What is it you are doing
there?"

"Oh, Papa," the son replied. "There is no need to worry. I go into the woods to pray. It is in the woods that I can talk to God."

"Oh," the rabbi said, clearly relieved. "But, as the son of a rabbi, you should know that God is the same everywhere."

"Yes, Papa. I know that God is the same everywhere. But, I am not."

This little boy knew, instinctively, that there are two spaces. Both of them important.

In the one space, we generate productivity, accomplishment, action, and busyness. It is a necessary space. And truthfully, I enjoy this space more than the other because I know who I am here. I get rewarded here—pats on the back, pay raises, compliments. And I find an odd comfort in playing that role.

In the other space we find quiet, reflection, prayer, contemplation, renewal, meditation, the power of pause, and, if we are lucky, unrepentant napping.

This second space is Sabbath space. Sabbath space is seldom encouraged in our we-want-it-now, are-you-keeping-busy, what-have-you-done-for-me-lately, are-you-somebody, super-size-that-please world.

I believe that deep down, all of us know the importance of Sabbath space. I also believe that all of us have such a space; we just don't know what to call it. The consequence? All too often we disregard it and don't give it the priority it deserves.

Your Sabbath space doesn't have to be the woods. It can be in your garden, in your car (while commuting), on a porch swing, by a lake or river, or at a fountain in the park. Sabbath space can be a particular corner of your home, a tucked-away spot in the library, or a chair in your favorite coffee shop.

Wherever that space may be, you and I can be grateful for the wisdom of a rabbi's young son. He knew that the key ingredient was not the actual physical space but who he was when he entered it.

"I go there," he told his father, "to listen."

Inspirations
God leads me to still waters, that restore my spirit.

—PSALM 23

A Powerful Pause for the Days Ahead
Find a space that helps you listen. In other words, find **your** Sabbath space.

3

Washing Dishes

Christ learned about his mission while he was cutting wood and making chairs, beds, and cabinets. He came as a carpenter to show us that—no matter what we do—everything can lead us to the experience of God's love.

—PAULO COELHO, *BY THE RIVER PIEDRA I SAT DOWN AND WEPT*

My friend Tim Hansel wrote a book on parenting. He asked his young sons, "Boys, how do you know Dad loves you?"

He figured that they would say, "Remember when you took us to Disney World, like for ten days!" They didn't say that.

He figured they'd say, "Remember the Christmas you bought us all that great stuff!"

They didn't say that. They said, "Dad, we know you love us when you wrestle with us."

He remembered two times. He had come home hungry, tired, and late. But these urchins were yanking on his pant leg.

"So I rolled with them on the floor, toward the kitchen," he said, "just to get them out of my way."

And then it hit him. In the middle of that very ordinary, boring event, real life was happening. Unfeigned joy, love, intimacy, connection, grace, sacrament—all were woven into the commonplace. "But," Tim laments, "I missed it. Because I was only tuned in to Disney World and Christmas."

There is nothing wrong with Disney World or Christmas. But they have meaning only because the sacred already resides in the more ordinary events and places. Because of the wrestling times.

God is real in small gifts and simple pleasures. God is present in the commonplace, the weak, the flawed, the compromised.

The profane is not the antithesis of the sacred, but the bearer of it.

We can get catawampus in our perspective when we split the world in two: the sacred and the nonsacred. Whenever I make that split, I find that I have done so because I am resentful or frustrated. I remember sitting in a Benedictine chapel for Compline. There was a lengthy—ten minutes or more—time of silence, for contemplation and reflection. But my mind raced with a conversation I had earlier that day. The conversation had been ugly and unpleasant. So I spent my ten minutes contemplating ways to get even, elaborate ways to make this person suffer. And then I felt guilty for wasting this time for spiritual reflection. My emotional turmoil and heat were only stoked by the need to move past this profane place. I was unable to allow it to also be a place of prayer.

We are so bent on removing ourselves from the mundane that we miss miracles. Not surprisingly, once we see the miracle in the mundane, we do our best to turn the mundane into a project: five steps to creating wrestling times. We do not rest in the solace that God is present, having nothing to do with our faith or our effort to invest the moment with meaning.

In other words, there is freedom in this gift of wrestling times. I don't need to craft the moment, I can simply live it.

I don't need to find meaning in the moment, I can receive it.

A monk once came to the Chinese Zen master Zhaozhou at breakfast time and said, "I have just entered this monastery to learn about God. Please teach me."

"Have you eaten your porridge yet?" asked Zhaozhou.

"Yes, I have," replied the monk.

"Then you had better wash your bowl."

~~~~~~

A Powerful Pause for the Days Ahead

This week, embrace the mundane acts, such as washing dishes, pulling weeds, commuting, walking the dog. Consider them a form of prayer.

4

The Gift of the Moon

Where there is no love, put love and you will find love.

—St. John of the Cross

Ryokan, a Zen master, lived the simplest kind of life in a small, remote hut. One night a thief entered the hut, only to discover there was nothing in it to steal. Ryokan returned and caught him in the act.

"You may have come a long way to visit me," he told the disillusioned prowler, "and you should not return empty-handed. Please take my clothes as a gift."

The thief was bewildered. But he took the clothes and crept back into the night.

Ryokan sat naked, watching the moon. "Poor fellow," he mused. "I wish I could have given him this beautiful moon."

Sometimes I feel like that thief. Standing—in my own home, or in front of an audience, or in a crowd, or all alone—and looking for something but, like that thief, not finding it. *What am I missing?* I ask myself. *What am I yearning for, that I find myself in such a pell-mell hurry?* So I run and call on God or the sky, or roll the dice with some prayer from my childhood. This will solve it. But the more I push, the more I ask, the more frustrated I become.

Here's the deal: In my state of distraction, I cannot see that the place where I stand right now—even without clarity or stability or faith—is right at the center of an awesome and illogical grace. Even as I wonder what I am looking for, I am smack-dab in the middle of the sacred present.

If I do have the freedom to see that place, I know that I am grounded. I can now breathe in, and out, and rest.

A week ago, my wife, son, and I left the house at predawn. I walked ahead of the car, pulling our garbage container down our drive to the main road. I happened to glance up to the eastern sky, where the moon was a slivered crescent, hanging on a deep royal blue sky. The sight was momentary, yet visceral and arresting. And for whatever reason, it was reassuring. I stopped. Literally, my legs quit moving. Now this snapshot was imprinted, and I knew in my heart that it was in some way vital and indispensable. I accepted this gift of the moon, even though I didn't yet know why.

As the day welcomes dawn, the sky on this morning is an enchanting pageant. The cloud cover is layered, like some sinfully rich marble cake. In other places, I see billowed fabric, with an occasional rent in the cloth, revealing the softest blue of morning sky. As the backlighting increases, the cloud formations become more substantial, as if a permanent, marbled sculpture. And the band of light just above the Cascade Mountains changes to a deep tangerine.

Yes, this scene is a tonic. There is something about these moments that carry significance. They are reminders, and they are sacraments—partial, yes, but containing the full sustenance of grace.

∾∾

Christmas tree lots are busy now, and stores have begun their exhortations to come and buy the perfect gift. (If you have a hankering, and money to spend, buy me an ugly tie and we'll call it good.)

In the church, we are about to begin the season of Advent. Advent is about waiting for the arrival of something or someone very important. (This is to be differentiated from Christmas, which is about waiting in line at the mall. And don't get me started about the parking lot, where I circled five times at Bellevue Square Mall, with my window rolled down, using salty language antithetical to Christmas cheer, shouting to the tune of "Jingle Bells.")

We are waiting for the arrival of something. But this is modern life, which tells us, "Stay very busy while you wait." Even in our churches we value busyness and create, in Thomas Kelly's words, "jitterbug programs of fevered activity." Advent schedules at a church offer three or four events per week. Even with so much to choose from, we feel, oddly, like that thief, empty-handed.

This reminds me of the young couple (a long time ago) who were looking for lodging. Their plans called for a semi-comfortable inn. What awaited them? An empty stable, with not much to offer but straw and starlight. And the songs of angels.

I wonder, what would happen if we made this announcement at church: "There are many activities this Advent. Because of that, we recommend you choose just one."

What are you doing this Advent? I'm sitting this one out. Really. After all, Advent is about waiting. As in sitting still.

Thinking of my predawn moment, I wish I could give you the gift of that crescent moon.

Inspirations

Be still and rest in the Lord; wait for Him and patiently lean yourself upon Him.

—PSALM 37

A Powerful Pause for the Days Ahead

Go look at the moon if you can. Stare at it and breathe in, breathe out. Think of this moonlight bathing your whole life—even the parts that are disorganized and unfinished.

5

New Rules

You cannot solve a problem with the same level of consciousness that created it.

—CARL JUNG, *THE UNDISCOVERED SELF*

A friend writes, "Dear Terry, You'd be happy to hear that about two weeks ago, someone cancelled a lunch and I found myself with an hour to spare. So I stopped, got a cup of coffee and actually didn't *read* or *write* or make *lists* or phone calls—I did nothing. And I don't think I have ever really done nothing that much (sounds like bad English, huh?); it was amazing. I felt so different after it (more relaxed, peaceful). And I finally 'got' what you say all the time. But this is my big question—How do you learn to continue to 'do nothing'? It's not so easy. I am trying to be intentional about it, but I have not been able to do it every day since then. Doing nothing might be one of the hardest things we can do. Have you written about that? Do you schedule an hour a day, like a meeting, to do nothing? Help!"

It is no surprise that we resonate with the challenging (and often onerous) obligation to stay perpetually preoccupied and productive. Our first inclination is always to ask, "What can we *do*?"

Terry, it would have been easier if you'd written a book called *Five Easy Steps to Powerful Pausing.*

Here's where the conversation about finding balance goes off the rails: Our Western mentality demands a resolution—answers. We know that we are stressed from having too much, doing too much, and feeling pressured by too much information. Our solution? We add something else to our lives.

Friend. . . . Are you overloaded? Overextended? Overtaxed? Overwhelmed? Then you need to *buy this*! We have ingested the notion that balanced living is about technique or strategy.

How much more straightforward it would all be if any spiritual/emotional growth predicament could be handled the way we deal with a stubborn union of plumbing pipe. Simply beat on it with a hammer. And mutter, of course, using language not encouraged by Baptist upbringing. My wife rolls her eyes. She is not familiar with the fine art of hammering enlightenment.

But when you think about it, adding one more thing to do—in order to relieve the stress of doing too much—is probably about as effective as my hammering on a pipe.

So, here's a new rule: let's face our problems by using a different process than the one that caused them. This goes against the grain, doesn't it? Is it possible that we change the way we live, not by addition, but by subtraction?

We can learn from the Amish. After the West Nickel Mines School shooting—when ten Amish children were shot, five of them killed, in their own schoolhouse—the Amish community began their healing process by forgiving the shooter and reaching out to the shooter's family (he took his own life, leaving behind his wife and children). The Amish attitude of forgiveness (shared by their entire community) was met with a mixture of awe, amazement, and respect. And, in some quarters, skepticism.

When asked about it, one Amish grandmother put it this way: "You mean some people actually thought we got together to plan forgiveness?" In other words, their behavior was not a plan, or strategy, or tactic, or ploy, or scheme, or device. It flowed from who they were, from the inside out.

It's our Western mind-set. We continue to think of spiritual and emotional growth in terms of a payoff, or cause and effect. If we do *this*, we reason, we will gain *thus and such*. We cannot see ourselves choosing for the sake of the thing (or event or activity or occasion or moment) itself. We need a payoff. We see this thinking in the rhetorical question we all hear (and ask) after any vacation, "Did you have fun?" It is not enough, apparently, just to go on vacation. While we are there, we need to produce fun.

This is not surprising in a world where we are pressed to be preoccupied with self-improvement. Our thinking goes this way

One—we resonate with the need to "sit still." To learn
how to pause and find moments of renewal.

Two—but, while we're at it, we want to learn to do it
correctly.

Three—and perhaps, even excel at it.

Four—who knows, some day there might be an Oscar
for best Sabbath performance.

Back to my friend's email. I answered: Cut yourself some slack. It is enough to keep the Sabbath, or a mini-Sabbath for that matter. Let it be enough. Give yourself permission to sit with, resonate in, and find solace from your time with coffee. Don't evaluate it, wondering whether it is correct or when the next opportunity will occur.

This is another way of saying, let yourself spend the time, this is a sensual moment. Because the sacrament of the sacred present always grounds us. Being present means that we are not thinking about the future payoff. We're noticing things. What do we hear, see, smell, taste, feel?

I'm not learning to pause in order to make me a more well-rounded or spiritual or balanced person. I don't even expect it to make me a better Christian.

Okay, yes. I will admit that in the strictest sense, there is a payoff. When I pause, when I practice Sabbath or mini-Sabbath, I do relax. My heartbeat slows. I am less at the mercy of the many things that crowd my mind and compete for my attention. In the words of a gardener, "When I get bogged down with life, I go into the garden, anchor myself to the earth, and let things wash over me. Gardening is wonderful therapy away from the pressures of life."

However, and this is an important however, let us be careful what we use for the measurement. When I was a kid, I participated from age ten to age seventeen in preaching contests. (Really—this is true.) And yes, I won them all. I was presented trophies, some enviable and saintly, some looking like bowling trophies. Even as youngsters, my friends and I would laugh, wondering when they were going to introduce prayer contests. Or even better, I wonder now, a Sabbath contest.

People frequently ask about Seattle weather. Mostly I fib. I say that it doesn't rain all that much. This past month, however, the weather has been mercurial. And our sky dark, and baleful. Today I have not yet finished everything on my (productivity) list. Regardless of my earlier observations, this breakdown adds a weight—some lament or need to apologize. Such cumbersome judgment requires drastic measures. I decide to leave my desk (and my list), and take a walk in my garden. All of the perennials have died back, waiting for spring. What remain are the garden bones, those plants evergreen through the winter months. In the front beds I take great pleasure in the nandina (heavenly bamboo) shrubs, with their pie-cherry red, butter yellow, and lime green leaves. They are encircled by, and highlighted by, black mondo grass. The backdrop is a combination of bronze flax, six feet tall with striking swordlike blades, and the comforting emerald green of an incense cedar. Our bluestone pathway glistens from the rain. The scene does my heart good and is soothing in its simple elegance.

Inspirations

Too often I looked at being relevant, popular, and powerful as ingredients of an effective ministry. Jesus sends us out to be shepherds and Jesus promises a life in which we increasingly have to stretch out our hand and be led to places where we would rather not go. He asks us to move from a concern for relevance . . . to a life of prayer, from worries about popularity . . . to communal and mutual ministry. . . . What is new is that we have moved from the many things, to the kingdom of God.

—HENRI NOUWEN,
IN THE NAME OF JESUS

~~~~~~

A Powerful Pause for the Days Ahead

Spend a day using a specific sense: hearing, sight, touch, taste, smell. That's all.

~~ **See** pictures of Terry's garden, by visiting www .loyolapress.com/powerofpause and clicking on Book Extras.

6

The Wonder of a Child

Children live in a world of dreams and imagination, a world of aliveness. . . . There is a voice of wonder and amazement inside all of us; but we grow to realize we can no longer hear it, and we live in silence. It isn't that God stopped speaking; it is that our lives became louder.

—MIKE YACONELLI, *DANGEROUS WONDER*

I heard the story about a father going through his five-year-old son's backpack and finding a picture of a little boy standing under a rainbow crying. His first thought was, "Oh God, my son is having some serious problems."

When he asked his son about the picture, the little boy told his father that he had been playing at school, and he saw a rainbow. "Dad," the little boy said, "the rainbow was so beautiful it made me cry."

The child is arrested by, absorbed in, beauty. Why? Because he has no restrictor plate in his soul.

I agree with Amy Rosenthal, who said, "If rainbows did not exist and someone said, 'Wouldn't it be cool to paint enormous stripes of color across the sky?' You'd say, 'Yes, that would be very cool—impossible, but very cool.' Children are totally tuned into the miracle of rainbows—that's why they are forever drawing them."

In the world of a child, awe precedes faith. In our adult world, we place a premium on belief (or belief systems) instead of awe. We put the cart before the horse. We see everything through our filters of judgment and evaluation. In doing that, we're removed from the experience itself—and from our emotions, yearnings, and prayers.

Jesus is unequivocal. "Unless you become like children, you will not experience the kingdom of Heaven." For children, wonderment grows in the soil of surprise. It is all about our capacity to receive.

My friend tells me the story about an ecumenical and integrated church service held in northern Louisiana. She attended the service with her priest. The service integrated black and white clergy of various denominations, including black Methodist and black Baptist preachers. It featured a choir from one of the local black Baptist churches.

For my friend, raised in Louisiana, having lived her life in a segregated world, this was a new and challenging experience. The service began, and she was wholly enthralled. She felt it, viscerally—the way the music lifted her up, nourishing and full of joy. It surrounded her and filled the sanctuary. It was her first experience in a church where she "gave in" to being enraptured.

Absorbing the music, inspired by the preaching, feeling a connection to the people around her—in pews filled with all manner of folk, mingled color and status, shared smiles and laughter—she told herself, "This is what heaven will be like." She let her tears flow freely.

In the car after, beginning the drive home, her priest said (in a tone undisguised), "Wasn't that positively dreadful?" He continued by listing all the problems and blunders with the liturgy, oblivious to the woman's joy. His words stung. She sat silent, assuming she had done something wrong to give in to such unadulterated joy.

We have moved from wonderment to consumption. It becomes the very antithesis of beauty. There is an attempt to Christianize it, by adding Jesus or God to the price tag. Eugene Peterson points out that in the end we have some kind of "spiritual self-help consumerism (lead, teach, garden, and cook like Jesus; 3, 4, 5, 10, or 21 laws, steps, or plans for the meaningful life), all of which leave us busier, more accomplished, but never filled."

We wean our children from wonder. I love the practice in Jewish tradition in which children are given a taste of honey during the celebration of the Torah. This is to remind them that the word of God is "sweet as honey" (Ezekiel 3:3).

"We teach children how to measure, how to weigh. We fail to teach them how to revere, how to sense wonder and awe."

—ABRAHAM HESCHEL,
BETWEEN GOD AND MAN

On the seventh day, God rested. God savored. Savoring is rooted in Sabbath. For six days we work, build, create, and control. The seventh day we rest. We stop. We receive. We savor. Without savoring, we assume that reality is only about what we create or produce. If we pay attention to this, there are three effects.

One, we are free to live this life. We are not driven to live another life, a different life. We find wonder here. As children, we find the kingdom of God, here.

There is a scene in the movie *The Shawshank Redemption* when Andy locks himself in the warden's office, puts a record on the turntable, and sets the prison intercom microphone near the speaker. The music, an aria from *The Marriage of Figaro*, pervades and suffuses the entire prison. Red, the narrator, says

I have no idea to this day what those two Italian ladies were singing about. Truth is, I don't want to know. Some things are best left unsaid. I'd like to think they were singing about something so beautiful, it can't be expressed in words, and makes your heart ache because of it. I tell you, those voices soared higher and farther than anybody in a gray place dares to dream. It was like some beautiful bird flapped into our drab little cage and made those walls dissolve away, and for the briefest of moments, every last man in Shawshank felt free.

Two, we savor beauty and resurrection in places we don't expect.

Another friend wrote, "I worked with my hands in the dirt, and it was saving me. The dirt was. How my hands felt digging. Gripping on the roots. The smells out there. The dark mornings. It made me feel stronger than I was. Because I had my hands on the earth. And the earth needed my hands, or so it seemed. And for those hours I didn't think much, or, if I did, the thoughts didn't feel as real."

Three, when I am present I am grateful. And gratitude is always a type of prayer.

I am riding the ferry from Seattle, on my way back to the island. Our winter ceiling has lifted today, and the entire region is bathed in sunshine. Now, at dusk, the cloud cover is scattered, like tattered pieces of cloth. Beyond the Olympic Mountains to the west, the sky is spring blue, baby boy blue. The Puget Sound water is ice blue and the mountains are blanketed with snow. In the clear winter air, the mountains stand stalwart—enduring, comforting, and settling. They are bigger than any of my pettiness. And their beauty slows my breathing and eases my mind. I had planned to finish writing about beauty, but the mountains enlighten me . . .

. . . it is enough just to sit, and savor.

Inspirations

Beauty has its purposes, which, all our lives and at every season, it is our opportunity, and our joy, to divine. . . . Much is revealed about a person by his or her passion, or indifference to this opening of the door of day.

—MARY OLIVER, *LONG LIFE*

A Powerful Pause for the Days Ahead

Do something this week that helps you sit in wonder. Write about your experience.

7

For Christmas: Joy to the World

Once again we find ourselves enmeshed in the Holiday Season, that very special time of year when we join with our loved ones in sharing centuries-old traditions such as trying to find a parking space at the mall. We traditionally do this in my family by driving around the parking lot until we see a shopper emerge from the mall, then we follow her, in very much the same spirit as the Three Wise Men, who 2,000 years ago followed a star, week after week, until it led them to a parking space.

—DAVE BARRY, *BOSTON GLOBE*
DECEMBER 6, 1987

A friend told me about the nativity play at her parish. A little girl played the role of the innkeeper. Mary and Joseph (Joseph resplendent in his dad's bathrobe) knocked on the door of the inn and asked, "Is there any room in your inn?"

The innkeeper looked at Mary and Joseph, and then looked out at the pastor. She looked again at Mary and Joseph, and then looked out at the pew where her parents sat. She looked again at Mary and Joseph, and said, "Oh well, come on in for a drink."

Now that's the spirit.

When Søren Kierkegaard wrote, "laughter is a type of prayer," I think he meant that with laughter, we give up our need to control or manage or manipulate. We allow ourselves the permission to receive the present situation, just as it is. This is easy to forget when we are compelled to do things "by number" or are constrained to feel a certain way. As Wayne Muller puts it in *Sabbath*, when we run headlong into Madison Avenue we hear, "Buy me. Do me. Watch me. Try me. Drink me. It is as if we have inadvertently stumbled into some horrific wonderland."

Yesterday, in the late afternoon, I overheard this exchange at the mall. A little girl, maybe six or seven years old, was waiting in line for Santa. She was, understandably, tired and a bit cranky. Her mother appeared to be close to the end of her own rope. The little girl slumped on the floor, and her mother squatted down near her. I heard the mother say, "Come on, get ready to smile for Santa. He doesn't have a lot of time, you know."

I wish I had leaned down to talk with the mother and daughter. I'd have said, "It's okay. I have a hard time smiling in a mall, too. And I just happen to know that this Santa has a lot of time. So, if it's okay, let me buy you both a hot chocolate."

Inspirations

Let us take a collective breath, rest, pray, meditate, walk, sing, eat and take time to share the unhurried company of those we love.

—WAYNE MULLER, *SABBATH*

~~~~~~

A Powerful Pause for the Days Ahead

This week, more than once if you can, take a deep breath. Let it out slowly. And have a peace-filled, everlasting, light-filled Christmas.

PART TWO

Late Winter

8

The Dark Side

The things that matter in a bad life, we know, are:
gaining power over others, accumulating as much stuff
as you can, getting revenge on your enemies (who are
everywhere), and drugging yourself one way or another
to forget the pain of not quite being human.

—GENE LOGSDON, *ALL FLESH IS GRASS*

I overheard this telephone conversation in an airport. A young
man, maybe age thirty, shouts into his cell phone, in a clearly
agitated voice, right arm gesticulating to no one in particular,
"Hey! Why didn't you return my call? I texted you. Like twenty
minutes ago."

Ah, the trials and tribulations of modern life. Not to mention the poignant inconvenience of having too many technically
challenged friends.

I did smile when I walked by our young impatient friend,
but I certainly claim no moral high road. I, too, have swallowed
the modern insistence on speed, instantaneous feedback, and an
utter disdain for wasted time. I know his feeling of agitation and

restlessness. I know what it feels like to shout (into a phone or into the air), my voice conveying how disgruntled I am. And I know what it is to quite literally feel the kindness, patience, compassion, and good-will-to-all-people leaching out of my soul.

Oddly enough, angry impatience feels good, in the way six cups of coffee feel good. There's that wired, teed off, on-pins-and-needles, irritated sort of energy that makes me ready to conquer the world, or at least the day. But I have no idea where to begin, or why.

When, precisely, did our expectations for instantaneous effect become a requirement for a life well lived? How did an unanswered phone message morph into a personal grievance?

Plato said, a long time ago, "What is honored in a country will be cultivated there." Much of what we honor (by our time, our focus, our energy, our priorities) is not conscious. In many ways we absorb this way of thinking—*without thinking*. These assumptions become a part of our life, a part of our reality. We assume that

- Busyness is a virtue and a sign of importance.
- Time spent waiting is wasted time.
- Going anywhere without a cell phone, or a way to be reached, is inconsiderate. (I've been curious: how many email messages—or spam—did Jesus have to sort through after his forty days in the desert?)
- Newer is ideal, and bigger is preferred.
- Multitasking is a spiritual gift.
- Rich people are those with money, and no time.

- Poor people are those with no money, and lots of time.
- Call-waiting is essential because the person calling me may be more important than the person I am speaking with now.

I am on a little working vacation. (Okay, I'm in Palm Springs, writing in the morning and lying by the pool in the afternoon, but that takes a lot of work.) The point of my trip: to get away from distractions in order to focus. So I had to laugh yesterday. I'm sitting at the pool, I hear a cell phone ring, and instinctively I reach for the table next to me. My phone is not there (apparently, it is not my phone ringing), but the way my mind and body are programmed made that move immediate and automatic. And what kind of call, pray tell, did I need to answer? What, exactly, was I afraid I would be missing if I didn't answer that call?

Technology is the easy whipping boy here. But that's not the point. The truth is that my insistence on speed—instant gratification—removes me from myself, and from the present.

And then I wonder; how did I get myself into this pickle? What have I been honoring here? And, if we absorb (or honor) these things without reflection, how can we change?

Let's go to the movies. Let's hang out with Luke Skywalker and draw on the insight of Yoda.

Yoda: Yes, a Jedi's strength flows from the Force. But beware of the dark side. Anger, fear, aggression; the dark side of the Force are they. Easily they flow, quick to join

you in a fight. If once you start down the dark path, forever will it dominate your destiny, consume you it will, as
it did Obi-Wan's apprentice.

Luke: Is the dark side stronger?

Yoda: No, no, no. Quicker, easier, more seductive.

Luke: But how am I to know the good side from
the bad?

Yoda: You will know . . . when you are calm, at peace,
passive.

I know this: I can't be calm or at peace if my multitasking
juices are flowing, or if I abhor any delay or I feel the need
to fill any vacuum. So the first step is to stop and take a deep
breath, and then to let it out very, very slowly and ask, "What
am I honoring here?"

I haven't thrown away my cell phone—not yet. But I did
turn it off for the afternoon. That's a start.

~~~~~~

A Powerful Pause for the Days Ahead

Go ahead and try it—turn off your cell phone for part of the day,
or even an entire day, or longer.

9

I'm Closed Now

You can't cut time with your tired scissors.

—PARAPHRASED FROM PABLO NERUDA'S

POEM, "TOO MANY NAMES"

Jesus is a publicist's nightmare. In the middle of his busy schedule (healing, teaching, and caring), with a lot of people clamoring for his attention ("and the whole town gathered at the door"), he withdraws—literally, withdraws—to a solitary place to pray.

His disciples, not understanding and feeling genuinely put out, hunt him down. When they find him, they exclaim, "Jesus, what are you doing here . . . doing *nothing*?!? Do you want to be a good Messiah, or not? Get back down there! People are counting on you. What will they think? Jesus, we need to get you to a time-management seminar. You could accomplish so much more!" (Actually, that's a *slightly* loose translation of Mark's Gospel.)

The literal translation sounds familiar, even to our modern ears: "Jesus, everyone is looking for you!" We've all heard some variation of this show of displeasure. Implying, "You have some nerve, saying *no*."

This way of thinking leads to two temptations. One, we begin to think that we derive our worth and value from what we do or produce. Therefore, we are motivated to be indispensable.

Two, we begin to see rest or Sabbath or withdrawing as wasteful and therefore guilt producing. ("Shouldn't you be doing something worthwhile with your time?")

The disciples said, "Everyone is looking for you."

Like I said, Jesus needs a spin doctor. Listen to his response: "Then let us go somewhere *else*."

Here's the bottom line: For Jesus, withdrawing is not optional. It is intentional and essential.

I give, relate, care, listen, and serve wholeheartedly if I am at home in my own skin. When I am in the hubbub of daily life, I can lose sight of that. I do so enjoy the adrenaline rush from being needed, and if I'm honest enough with myself, I recognize that adrenaline is addictive. I know that when I give in to the "should" of being all things to all people, and when I give up the need to withdraw for rest and renewal, I lose the rhythm of life that feeds my soul.

In withdrawing, Jesus is saying to his disciples, "Do you see that clump of people? Do you know why I have any power in that clump? Because I regularly say *no*, to withdraw to a place where I listen to a different voice—my Father's voice—about my identity."

I know from personal experience that if I don't say no, no will be said for me by default, and I will end up saying no to the people I love the most.

The story goes that when Dwight Eisenhower was president, he stood at a meeting of the cabinet and said, "This meeting is adjourned."

"But Mr. President, there is still much work to be done. We need to extend the meeting."

"The meeting is adjourned because I promised my grandson I would play football with him at 3:30. It is 3:30."

"But Mr. President, some of this business cannot wait."

"Gentlemen, I can give you reasons why we are adjourning. I could never offer a good reason to my grandson why I would miss my commitment to play football."

We miss the point if we see this as a means to an end. I'll rest so that I'll be more productive when I return; I'll be rewarded; I'll benefit. As if we can manufacture meaning by how we orchestrate our lives.

We miss the point if we assume that the power of Sabbath is in the program or method. Whether we choose meditation, observing Shabbat, walking the dog, Centering Prayer, soaking in a hot bath, practicing yoga, praying the Divine Hours, joining in Taize prayer, walking a labyrinth, or napping in a hammock for the afternoon, it is enough to withdraw. The power of the story in the Gospel of Mark is the verb *withdrew*. There is nothing overtly spiritual or spectacular here. It is simply a sign on the door of the soul: "I'm closed now."

I love Susan Shaw's take on all of this.

The most helpful thing I grasped while waitressing was that some tables are my responsibility and some are not. A waitress gets overwhelmed if she has too many tables, and no one gets good service. In my life, I have certain things to take care of: my children, my relationships, my work, one or two causes, and myself. That's it. Other things are not my table. I would go nuts if I tried to take care of everyone, if I tried to make everybody do the right thing. If I went through my life without ever learning to say, "Sorry, that's not my table, Hon," I would burn out and be no good to anybody. I need to have a surly waitress inside myself that I can call on when it seems everyone in the world is waving an empty coffee cup in my direction. My Inner Waitress looks over at them, keeping her six plates balanced and her feet moving, and says, "Sorry, Hon, not my table."

Inspirations

And Jesus withdrew to a solitary place to pray.

—THE GOSPEL OF MARK

A Powerful Pause for the Days Ahead

Find a way to withdraw for at least half a day. No phone. No email. No errands and no visits. If you're brave, wear some form of "I'm Closed" sign—a lapel pin or a variation on a nametag.

10

Changing the Questions

Our whole business therefore in this life, is to restore to health the eyes of the heart whereby God may be seen.

—ST. AUGUSTINE, *CONFESSIONS*

Writer Natalie Goldberg lived in Jerusalem for three months and, in her book *Writing Down the Bones*, shares this story about her Israeli landlady, a woman in her fifties. Her landlady had called a repairman to fix a broken TV. It took the repairman four visits to fix the screen.

"But you knew even before he came the first time what was wrong," Natalie told her. "He could have brought the correct tube and fixed it immediately."

The landlady looked at her in astonishment. "Yes, but then we couldn't have had a relationship, sat and drunk tea during the second and third and fourth visit to discuss the progress of the repairs."

Of course, Goldberg writes, the goal was not to fix the machine but to have a relationship.

We think of measurement as a requisite skill set. Even with Sabbath moments, when I have spent the afternoon in my garden, I am prone to ask, "What did I achieve? What did I accomplish? Was it successful?" Even with Sabbath, I want to "do it" correctly, as if there's a manual of Sabbath keeping and God is an Olympic judge.

I need permission to change the questions. As the Little Prince discovered

> If you were to say to the grown-ups: "I saw a beautiful house made of rosy brick, with geraniums in the windows and doves on the roof," they would not be able to get any idea of that house at all.
>
> You would have to say to them: "I saw a house that cost $20,000." Then they would exclaim: "Oh, what a pretty house that is!"

I was asked, just a little while ago, "Did you have a good day?" Instead of a knee-jerk response, I paused and did the mental math. Good day? Did it measure up? Did it stay on script? Did it go off script? What did I add to my life today? And what did I let go of? Realizing that the person who asked the question was staring at me, as if I had vacated earth, I answered, "Oh yes, thanks for asking."

And I think back to Natalie Goldberg's story. And her landlady's openness to allow the day to unfold. She had no preconditions as to whether the day measured up. And in that place, she shared a cup of tea with a new friend.

A Powerful Pause in the Days Ahead

What are the characteristics of a "good day" for you?

~~~ **Visit** www.loyolapress.com/powerofpause and click on Book Extras to create and print a "good day" card. Place the card somewhere you will see it often to serve as a reminder of the daily graces in your life.

11

Dragons Can Be Pink

This is the categorical imperative of the Christian Faith: You shall lovingly accept the humanity entrusted to you. You must not continually try to escape it.

—JOHANNES METZ, *POVERTY OF SPIRIT*

Lovingly accept the humanity entrusted to you.

This is not so easily accomplished in a world that dotes on vicarious lives, where the role of the article and the ads in the magazine I peruse in the hotel lobby is to make me feel unhappy, inadequate, and insufficient. (Whoever is responsible for this magazine must be good at what they do, because they accomplished their goal.)

In a friend's house I see a crayon picture of a dragon that is pink, purple, and lavender. I like this dragon and say so.

"My daughter drew that when she was very young," says my friend. "And her teacher told her that she'd done it all wrong. Everyone knows that dragons are not *that* color!"

It starts early, doesn't it? *Don't be different. What will people think? Please don't embarrass me. No one wants to hear your opinion.*

As a youngster—in school, at church, in the family—I expended enormous amounts of energy trying to be the right kind of kid. Sensitive to adult displeasure, I always found a way to adapt. Needless to say, my dragons were never pink.

In the movie *Benny and Joon*, a quirky guy named Sam spends time in the home of Benny and his younger sister, Joon. In one scene in a local park, Sam begins to entertain them with a Buster Keatonesque routine using his hat and cane. Soon a crowd gathers, fully entertained and appreciative.

"That was great," says Benny. "Did you learn that in school?"

"No," says Sam. "I was kicked out of school for that."

There will always be someone telling you that you're not enough. But if you play to such voices, you'll sacrifice your emotions, gifts, passions, and unique humanity. God wants *you*, not your version of someone else.

So, what color is your dragon today?

Inspirations

Nathaniel (speaking about Jesus) said to Philip, "Can any good thing come out of Nazareth?" Philip said to him, "Come and see."

—THE GOSPEL OF JOHN

A Powerful Pause for the Days Ahead

Read this quote every day this week, and let it work on your soul.

> "You shall lovingly accept the humanity entrusted to you."

12

Simplicity

It is always the simple things that change our lives. And these things never happen when you are looking for them to happen. Life will reveal answers at the pace life wishes to do so. You feel like running, but life is on a stroll. This is how God does things.

—DONALD MILLER, *BLUE LIKE JAZZ*

It's snowing here. Outside our kitchen window, the sky is filled with a flotilla of tiny parachutes, floating quietly from the heavens. These are whopping snowflakes (I think that is the technical term), and as the snow clings to the bare branches of hydrangea and viburnum, I can't decide if I'm seeing cotton balls or small scraps of fabric.

"We're going to have a winter wonderland," Zach tells whomever is listening. "It's time to go sledding." It is no use pointing out the obvious to a ten-year-old; there is not yet any snow on the ground.

Exactly one year ago, a snowstorm crippled the region. No electricity, trees down, roads turned to black ice. Plans—whatever they may have been, or for whatever length of time they had been on our calendars—changed. We hunkered down in our houses. This is the weather when one is given to introspection. Or hot chocolate. Or a hot toddy. Or all three.

Our storms make folks in Denver or Buffalo or Michigan's Upper Peninsula shake their heads and snicker. "You call that snow? That's just a few flurries, son."

This year, it's not the crippling kind of storm, but even so, hunkering down seemed a good idea, so I spent some time going through a stack of magazines that had been accumulating. I started with an excerpt from a book about relaxing. "Cleaning is overrated," the author says. He believes that laziness and sloppiness can be a good way to save time. He'll get no argument from me, but I had to laugh. We're such a driven culture (requiring productivity) that it isn't enough to be lazy for its own sake. Now there needs to be a payoff—in this case, saving time.

I perused another article about people who have shunned cell phones. "They will find me if they need me," said one man. The article quoted a lawyer who practices Shabbat, turning off his cell phone and computer and email on Friday at sundown.

He's got the right idea.

And that part resonates with all of us: *simplify.*

We're on the same page. Except that the next thing you know, we make an assignment and duty out of it, as if there will be a test.

And Jesus said, "Blessed are the poor in spirit." And Simon Peter said, "Do we have to write this down?"

In the end, what happens? We focus on the endeavor of simplifying, instead of . . . well . . . just simplifying. (Or, in the words of Guillaume Apollinaire, "Now and then it's good to pause in our pursuit of happiness and just be happy.")

There is a cartoon about two monks sitting in meditation. The older monk is responding to a question from the novice monk. "Nothing happens next. This is it."

I heard a great story about an older man who, every day after work, stopped at a church in the late afternoon. The man would sit in the back pew for a good bit of time, sitting still and silent, looking straight ahead. After time had passed, the man would get up and leave. The parish curate was quite puzzled by this regular visitor. One day he decided to ask. "I'm wondering, sir, why you come here. You have no prayer book. You have no Bible. You carry no rosary. You don't appear to be praying—what are you doing?"

The man answered, "Well, I come here every afternoon, usually after a long and tiring day. I stop here to pray. So I just sit here and look at Him, and while I'm sitting here, He just looks at me."

Looking for insight in all of this is a good way to miss the moment. Just think of it—you never see a child step back from playing and say, "Oh, so that's what I experienced."

In last year's blizzard, we needed to take the afternoon ferry from Seattle to our island. I was cold and ornery. Zach was shuffling along in the snow, past a cluster of waiting commuters standing close together for warmth. They reminded me of a waddle of penguins, huddled and somber. Zach was kicking snow, oblivious to the downside of this weather or this moment. He repeated, over and over, "This is so great. This is soooo great."

We simplify our lives not by theory or a seven-step program for life management. We simplify when we follow the example of the old man in the back pew. When we sit a spell.

Why? Because sitting allows us to *see*. Rilke once wrote of how he learned to stand "more seeingly" in front of certain paintings. That's what I want. To live this moment more "seeingly."

Mary Oliver talks about "naming" with her poetry. "I am fascinated with naming. This is, specific names, the exact right word for things. Yes, naming suggests a kind of power, even if false or fleeting, but naming also praises, honors, celebrates." It is what writer Frank O'Connor referred to when he said that the "moral basis of poetry is the accurate naming of the things of God."

It's been snowing steadily for some hours now. We have about four inches of snow on the ground. Zach's been knocking on my study window for the past fifteen minutes, needing me to drive him up the road to a great sledding hill. I keep telling him, "In a minute, son, Dad's busy." I could tell him about simplicity, and life being pared down to the essentials and non-negotiables, and about my insights for this current writing project.

Or, I can take him sledding. Insight can wait. Now it's time to kick the snow.

～～～～～～～～～～～～～～～～～～～～～

A Powerful Pause for the Days Ahead

Find a place where you can sit and look at God, and God can look at you.

13

Unreasonable Grace

The greatest things in life are not reasonable. The mind may make sensible comments about these greatest things in life, but they are not reasonable. The love of a mother for her child has reason, but it is not reasonable. The love of a man for a woman, and the other way around, is surely not reasonable. Beauty, a sunset, the great plunging torrents of Niagara, the final tremendous thunders of the Hallelujahs in Handel's Messiah, *the catch in the throat when the sun sets over the sea striking a line of gold on the calm waters, touches us at a different level from logic and reason. And the love of God for us is not reasonable.*

—REV. GARDNER TAYLOR, ATTRIBUTED

In her story "The Whisper Test," Mary Ann Bird relates that she grew up knowing she was different, and she hated it. Mary was born with a cleft palate. She would hear the jokes and tolerate the stares of other children—some cruel, others simply curious—who teased her about her misshapen lip, her crooked nose, and garbled speech. Mary grew up hating the fact that she was different. She was convinced that no one outside her family could ever love her.

Until she entered Mrs. Leonard's class. Mrs. Leonard had a warm smile, a round face, and shiny brown hair.

In the 1950s, teachers would administer an annual hearing test. In addition to her cleft palate, Mary was able to hear out of only one ear. Determined not to give classmates another difference to tease, each year she would cheat on the hearing test.

It was called the whisper test. The teacher would stand one to two feet behind the student so that the child could not read her lips. The student would place one finger on the opposite ear to obscure any sound. The teacher would whisper toward the student's ear words with two distinct syllables. The student would repeat the phrase to the teacher. When Mary turned her bad ear toward her teacher, she always pretended to cover her good ear. Mary knew that teachers would typically say, "The sky is blue" or "What color are your shoes?" But not on that day. Mrs. Leonard changed Mary's life forever. When the whisper test came, the child heard these words: "Mary, I wish you were my little girl."

Unreasonable grace doesn't make sense. I'm sure little Mary wondered why anyone would want her for a child. Unreasonable grace stops us cold because we weren't expecting it, or even looking for it. It's grace that finds you on an ordinary day, maybe with a cup of coffee in your hand looking out the window at a rain-leaden sky—when you notice a narrow shaft of sunlight illuminating the ground near a moss-covered log where a cluster of daffodil shoots defies winter and sprouts from the soil.

And because we don't expect this kind of grace, we usually miss it because we rushed through a moment. We didn't look out the window long enough to see those daffodil shoots. We didn't pause long enough to hear someone say, "I love you" or "You really are amazing."

Inspirations

God does not die on the day when we cease to believe in a personal deity, but we die on the day when our lives cease to be illumined by the steady radiance, renewed daily, of a wonder, the source of which is beyond all reason.

—DAG HAMMARSKJOLD, *MARKINGS*

A Powerful Pause for the Days Ahead

What is your whisper test? Who, or what, might be speaking grace to you right now?

PART THREE

Early Spring

14

Broken and Crippled

What we have brought to the Sabbath Dance and what God has brought in return. It is not now, nor will it ever be, a fair exchange. We bring our brokenness; some of it we can hardly bear to name, some of it we cannot name at all. God brings forgetfulness, so that it might never again be named. If we will let it go, then we will be empty, we will be clean, we will have room in our hearts for the Word.

—ROBERT BENSON, *BETWEEN THE DREAMING AND THE COMING TRUE*

Seeing the sign, Puppies for Sale, a little boy asked the store owner, "How much are you asking for those puppies?"

"Fifty dollars each."

The boy emptied his pocket. "I have $2.37—can I have a look at them?"

The storeowner whistled, and out came Lady, followed by five balls of four-legged fur. One puppy limped and lagged considerably. "What's wrong with that one?" the boy asked.

"He was born without a hip socket. The vet says he'll limp for the rest of his life."

The boy's face lit up. "That's the puppy I want to buy!"

"If you really want him, I'll give him to you."

"I don't want you to give him to me," said the boy, annoyed. "He's worth every penny. I'd like to give you $2.37 now and fifty cents every month until he's paid for."

"Young man, this puppy is never going to be able to run, jump, or play!"

The boy rolled up his pant leg to reveal a badly twisted, crippled leg supported by a bulky metal brace. "Well, I don't run so well myself, and this puppy will need someone who understands."

In *Brendan*, Frederick Buechner's novel about a sixth-century Irish saint, a servant recounts a conversation between Brendan and Gildas, a crippled and bitter old priest.

"I'm as crippled as the dark world," Gildas said.

"If it comes to that, which one of us isn't my dear?" Brendan said.

Gildas with but one leg. Brendan sure he'd misspent his whole life entirely. Me that had left my wife to follow him and buried our only boy. The truth of what Brendan said stopped all our mouths. We was cripples all of us. . . .

"To lend each other a hand when we're falling," Brendan said. "Perhaps that's the only work that matters in the end."

We all see "crippled" parts of ourselves that sadden, discourage, infuriate, embarrass, or even repulse us. We know they are there. Some are of our own making, but most are not. And we do our best to wish or will or pray them away.

Our prayers are fueled by a world that sees imperfection as an indictment. And we pass judgment on our value, based upon that measurement. Maybe it's about our illusion of control. With all our fixing and renovating, look what we have to show for ourselves! "You can have the life you *deserve* to live," an ad for a local plastic surgeon promises. I have nothing against whiter teeth or a tighter backside. However, I'm not so sure that'll take care of what troubles me.

The problem is, as long as I'm bent on fixing, repairing, and renovating in order to make myself more presentable or lovable or acceptable, I am postponing the ability to receive any gifts (from you or from God) in the moment I have right now. One young volunteer, working at L'Arche, Jean Vanier's homes for seriously handicapped adults, said of the residents. "They never ask what degree do you have, what university did you attend. They only ask, 'Do you love me?' And in the end, isn't that what matters?" (www.larchejacksonville.org)

Indeed. We have the ability to receive, to be loved, to know our value—only from a place of vulnerability. Because in our nakedness, our crippledness, our brokenness and our vulnerability, we have no power, no leverage, nothing to bargain with. Our identity is not dependent upon becoming somebody, impressing somebody, or removing all imperfection. We can be—literally *be*—at home in our own skin, damaged hip socket and all.

I was raised in a church that used the scripture, "Be ye perfect as God is perfect," as a hammer meant to beat all the blemishes out of me. Now I know that wholeness is not perfection. Wholeness is embodying—living in—this moment, be it happy or sad, full or empty, running or limping.

I know what it feels like to stand before an audience—exhausted, parts of me fragile and wanting to break—and still spending energy putting on a "together" exterior. It is not easy to ignore the internal pressure to hide how much I'm hurting.

Granted, there are flawed and weak parts that could change. But we can't change anything until we can love it. We can't love anything until we can know it. We can't know anything until we can embrace it.

And we touch wholeness at that place of vulnerability. There we are human. There we are sons and daughters of God. There we hear God speak our name. The very image of God is imbedded in this fragile nature, in its very breakability. It is in that vulnerability where we find exquisite beauty: compassion, tenderheartedness, mercy, forgiveness, gentleness, openness, kindness, empathy, listening, understanding, and hospitality. The alternative? To protect ourselves from all manner of breakability and crippledness and to seal off our hearts and souls.

In that sealed-off place, there will be no pain or brokenness. And there will be no love.

A Powerful Pause for the Days Ahead

Read some Psalms out loud. I recommend Psalm 51 and Psalm 34. Connect with the brokenness of the psalmist, and let those words be expressions of your life now.

15

Pause Button

You are now running on reserve power and your screen has been dimmed. You will be able to continue working for a short time. Please plug in your power adapter to begin recharging the battery. OK?

—MESSAGE ON MY APPLE COMPUTER
POWERBOOK SCREEN

On an Ohio spring afternoon, bright lemony light slants through an open window, into the kitchen where five-year-old Katy is making cookies with her mother. Birds sing in the distance.

Katy says, "Shh, Mom, listen."

"What, Katy?"

"Shh, listen," the child insists.

"What am I listening to?" asks her Mom.

"If you are quiet and listen, you can hear God talking to us."

It's tempting to focus on some potential payoff: What did God say? And what's in it for me?

Or on the impediment: Why can't I hear God? And if I can't, can someone please give me the secret code? There are plenty of well-meaning folks—and some not so well-meaning—who boast of some direct line to God: "God told me to say . . ." I guess I'm glad for them. But if God talks to them so much, why do they so often appear self-important? And while I'm wondering, why is it that the people who claim to be closest to God, seem to laugh the least?

The wisdom of this child is unadorned. Only two words: "Shh, listen."

Shh requires stopping. Sitting still. And something even more inconvenient: waiting. There's no getting around the truth that we find wisdom (insight, understanding, acceptance) in pushing the pause button.

This doesn't sit well with us usually because we are wired for closure. Like four-year-old children five minutes out of the driveway, on any family trip. "Are we there yet?" "Are we done now?" We want to "get somewhere," or at least add fuel to our guilt about not getting somewhere—not being where we *should* be.

The truth is, if we were in charge, there would be no waiting allowed. Because waiting doesn't *do* anything. Plus it wastes valuable time. And, quite frankly, it's not good for my blood pressure. It's exasperating and makes me do things I regret, like devouring the *People* magazine in my doctor's waiting area. Besides, we all know that the good life is about activity, excitement, achievement, goings-on, urgency, and getting things done. Waiting is a tribulation that must be avoided at all cost.

But what if?

What if the pause button—*shh*, listen!—is not about achieving anything? What if it's about receiving?

What if it's about embracing the day—this day, this moment—as a gift?

What if it's enough to allow love to break through to that place in our soul that is blocked by busyness, self-importance, self-indulgence, and self-pity?

To wait, to listen, to discern—*discernere*. The pause that allows us to separate, to distinguish, to sift through. Throughout the centuries, teachers have reminded us of this in different ways. Meister Eckhart wrote that we must "go into [our] own ground" of silence "and learn to know [ourselves] there." St. John of the Cross called it "hearing silent music," for only in silence can we hear God speaking to our soul. The psalmist was brief: "Be still and know." For St. Elizabeth of the Trinity, silence enabled God to create a beloved solitude within the soul.

We could all learn from the old guy sitting on his front porch in his rocking chair, rocking and smoking his pipe. A group of young people passes by, and one of them calls out, "Hey old man, what are you doing?" The man rocks and smokes for a minute and then says, "How soon do ya need to know?"

The ferry ride from Seattle to Vashon Island is a pause button, because it takes away my control over time. It is dusk in late March. The sun is setting, now out of sight behind the Olympic Mountains. The mountains are a work of art, rendered in deep charcoal. Against the cool blue sky, the outline of their peaks is precise, as if drawn with a fine-point lead pencil. In that precision, that demarcation, there is something evocative, and it resonates deep inside. I see the very breath of God, as if I am responding to a kindred spirit, knowing that these mountains, too, like me, are the very breath of God. My response is visceral, a nod of the head, and my heart wells up. I uncover no answers or instructions, nor even any certainty about my questions, but this I know: any urgency tugging at my heart, recedes. And I know that in waiting, listening, I am tethered to this present moment without any need for resolution.

However, and wherever, you pause—*shh*, listen! You might just hear God talking.

~~~~~~~~~~~~~~~~~~~~~~~~~~~~~~~~~~~~~~~

A Powerful Pause for the Days Ahead

Buy a flower, pick a flower, have a cup of coffee, watch people, sit in a park, visit a beach, close your eyes while on the commuter train or bus . . .

Allow for extra time while you're driving. Take a different route, one that allows you to drive slowly. Notice things along this route. If you see something interesting, stop and investigate.

~~~ **Discover** some of America's most captivating driving routes. Visit www.byways.org and browse the list of National Scenic Byways.

16

Duckling Moments

People travel to wonder at the height of mountains, at the huge waves in the sea, at the long courses of rivers, at the vast compass of the ocean, at the circular motion of the stars; and they pass by themselves without wondering.

— ST. AUGUSTINE, COMMENTARY ON
SERMON ON THE MOUNT

I heard this story from a friend. The young couple stood in the ticket line at Knott's Berry Farm. Between the ticket kiosk and the main gate their two young boys—maybe ages five and six—were passing the time playing, waiting for their parents. Their focus of attention: a family of Mallard ducks. A mom, dad, and several new ducklings. Because the ducks lived at the theme park, they were untroubled by the presence of people. The boys were flat on their bellies, eye to eye with the ducklings, captivated and giggling. With tickets finally in hand, the parents walked up to find their boys on the pavement.

They were overheard saying, loudly, "Boys, get up off of there. We've got to get into the park and start having fun."

Every day, we are bombarded with the same insistent injunction, with the implication that life begins elsewhere. And we miss the "duckling moments."

We do set ourselves up to live this way. I have no doubt that the young parents were unaware of their temporary blinders. We have been trained to see that which is beyond the moment—to that which is more exciting, yet to come, the next best thing. When I'm watching a football game on TV, there are frequent ads for upcoming games (a week or two in the future), using the enticement, "This is the game we've all been waiting for." It subtly (well, not so subtly) takes root, rendering the game I am watching at this moment not so important after all. "I can't wait until next week. It's going to be a great game."

Rediscovering wonder (or duckling moments) takes root in the soil of the simple sentence, "I never noticed that before." I am inviting life in, not allowing internal censors and judges to scrutinize to make certain this moment passes muster. In moments of amazement, we render our internal scorekeeper mute.

It appears that some people get all the moments of astonishment. But maybe, like these young boys, they've allowed themselves to see. Either way, these moments sustain us.

Inspirations

Dear Lord, grant me the grace of wonder. Surprise me, amaze me, awe me in every crevice of Your universe. . . . Each day enrapture me with Your marvelous things without number. I do not ask to see the reason for it all; I ask only to share the wonder of it all.

— ABRAHAM HESCHEL

～～～～～～～～～～～～～～～～～～～～～～

A Powerful Pause in the Days Ahead

Remember one of your own "duckling moments." Look for one this week, and then tell someone about it.

Instead of asking people, "What did you do?" ask about their duckling moments.

17

Bless Me

Sometimes in life we have to become less to be more. We become whole people, not on the basis of what we accumulate, but by getting rid of everything that is not really us, everything false and inauthentic.

—HAROLD KUSHNER, *WHEN ALL YOU'VE EVER WANTED ISN'T ENOUGH*

I remember a *M*A*S*H** episode (Season 4, "Quo Vadis, Captain Chandler?") in which a wounded bombardier thinks he is Jesus. The camp is mixed. Some say he's crazy; most say he's putting on an act in order to get discharged from the army.

One person in camp believes him: Radar.

When it's time for the man's release, Radar walks out to the jeep where the man sits. "Excuse me, Jesus, sir. Could you bless my friend?"

"Yes."

And Radar pulls his teddy bear from behind his back. Jesus blesses the bear.

"Excuse me, Jesus, sir. Could you bless me?"

"Yes, Radar."

Radar steps back in deference. "Thank you. And my name. It's not Radar, sir. It's Walter."

Bless me.

What is he asking for? Most definitions say that to be blessed is to be granted God's favor and protection, or that blessing means the bringing of pleasure or relief. Blessing is like that exhalation from someplace deep inside that means: "I am well, all is well."

This is good news in a world where we are bombarded by the need to achieve, or pursue, and we are rewarded by having more, or by being *somebody*. There are those who use blessing to seek personal gain. As if it is about what we own.

To be blessed is to know that place of no striving.

To be blessed is to know that place of rest.

To be blessed is to know that I am loved by a gracious Creator, and that I can own and celebrate my identity, knowing that it is enough.

And it all begins, simply, with the affirmation of my name.

In the Gospel of John, Mary is looking for Jesus. He's not where he is supposed to be (in the grave). She is weeping, having lost what she needed for stability.

She sees a man, whom she assumes is the gardener, and asks, "Please tell me where you've put him."

And the man says only one word: "Mary." By that one word, Mary knows that it's Jesus. And in that word, in her name, is the blessing.

The blessing is the permission to be. Without the need for absolute security, or certainty, or striving.

So, bless me. Not for what I've done or failed to do. But for who I am. Mary. Walter. (Your name). Loved by God.

I had such a moment today. After a long weekend of teaching and preaching, I slept on Cayucos Beach, on the central California coast. There are times after a weekend when I give in to second-guessing: Did I do enough? Did I say enough? Was I helpful enough?

But not today. Today I slept on the sand and listened to the wind. I knew that my identity rested in the hands of a loving and faithful Creator.

And my striving ceased. I was blessed indeed.

A Powerful Pause for the Days Ahead

Sit in a quiet place and ask God to bless you. Be sure to say your name aloud—not for God to hear, but for you.

18

Full

Every family should have a peaceful space or breathing room, where any member can take refuge.

—THICH NHAT HANH, *CREATING TRUE PEACE*

An important businessman, hurried and stressed, visits a Zen master, seeking guidance. The Zen master sits down, invites the businessman to sit, and pours the visitor a cup of tea. But even after the tea fills the cup, the Zen master continues to pour, allowing the tea to spill, now running over the entire table.

The businessman is taken aback. "Stop! Please stop pouring the tea! The cup is full and obviously can't hold any more."

The Zen master replies, "Yes. So it is with you. And you will not be able to receive any guidance unless you make some empty space first."

When I read that story, I had to nod. I can relate to the businessman. And yet there's something alluring about filling an empty space. Just recently I said yes to a speaking job, not because I needed it or wanted it, but because the space on my calendar glared at me as if to say, "What do you mean, you have nothing?"

We live in a world that abhors an empty space. If we find one, we feel compelled to fill it. One thing I know: When there is no empty space, we pay the price. I am full. Stuffed. Numb. When my senses are numbed by noise and overload, I am impoverished. I become a man who, in the words of Leonardo da Vinci, "looks without seeing, listens without hearing, touches without feeling, eats without tasting, moves without physical awareness, inhales without awareness of odour or fragrance, and talks without thinking."

Here's the catch. Slowing down. Stopping. Making space. Saying no. It is a form of civil disobedience.

Why? Because it goes against the grain.

When Mary was given the word that she was carrying Jesus, it says she "kept all these things and pondered them in her heart."

In other words, she made space.

Here's what it doesn't say: And Mary figured it all out. And Mary wrote a book on the Seven Lessons from an Angel's Visit. And Mary filled her calendar and traveled all over Galilee doing seminars about successful living.

Here is the power of space. With space we are able to receive, and our lives are fueled by gratitude.

Inspirations

I find that God made man simple; man's complex problems are of his own devising.

—ECCLESIASTES

A Powerful Pause for the Days Ahead

Spend some time with your calendar and planner—and *take off* at least one item from this week's list.

19

Damage Control

Man is born broken. He lives by mending. The grace of God is the glue.

—ATTRIBUTED TO EUGENE O'NEILL

A rabbi visited a young couple who had lost a child. He waxed eloquent from the Scriptures about loss and grief and God and pain and God's will and about enduring distress. For two hours he explained the theology of pain to them. And in the end he asked, "So, would you like me to explain it again?"

"No, thank you, Rabbi," answered the young man. "We have already suffered enough!"

I grew up in a religious tradition that knew what to say in bad times, broken times, grieving times, wounded times. People had Bible verses for me. They were our designated "Bible verse spouters." It seemed to be a spiritual gift—these people had answers. In each case, I was told that my situation was a problem to be solved, not a mystery to be embraced.

I would hear these pronouncements and feel, at the very least, dense or, more likely, void of faith because apparently I didn't get it.

The truth was, there were still times when I felt lost, lonely, wounded, hurt, tired, or disillusioned. And for some reason I couldn't make the formula work. These answers did not give me peace. They just made me want to hit someone.

Reminds me of a cartoon. Two men walk to the top of a sacred mountain to talk with a great guru.

"Life is like a river," says the guru.

"You've got to be kidding," say the men. They begin to choke the guru.

"Okay, okay," says the guru. "Life is not like a river."

We all agree on this. Life is difficult.

And some of us—no, all of us—break. Maybe from boredom, or lack of passion, or illusion of familiarity, or loss of childlikeness, or fatigue of spirit, or cruelty, or despair.

A woman visited my house today and walked in the garden with me. Her son, age twenty-four, was killed in an accident earlier this year. The loss still weighs heavily on her. None of the equations that come as standard equipment in our brains seem adequate. Children are not supposed to die before their parents.

She tells me that she has any number of people, including good friends, who tell her the goal is to move on. Get over the grief.

I tell her that I didn't know that was the goal. If it is, I tell her, it's not a good one.

Another friend tells me she thinks she is going crazy.

And another is sad in his marriage and tells me life isn't fun anymore.

We live in a crazy, interior war of our own expectations. One of the hardest things to accept is the way our life has gone. We tell ourselves that things should have turned out differently. Or in the words of Captain Jack Aubrey in the movie *Master and Commander*, "Not all of us become the men we once hoped we might be."

And then, once we recognize this, we try to compensate. For instance, I keep myself busier and work even harder to impress others. Which means that it's all about whether I matter. Maybe deep down I don't want to be original, I just want to be liked. Or admired. Or appreciated. Or just noticed. But I've got to matter somehow.

By trying to compensate for the fact that I'm broken, or that I don't matter enough, I spend too much of my energy running from my life. I assume that answers are down the road, or around the corner, or buried in some Bible verse. If there is any unease or mess or brokenness, I spend a good deal of fuel—mental, spiritual, and physical energy—trying to appease it, dampen it, control it, or manage it. Like some political damage-control public-relations campaign. I may be a mess, but I don't want people to see it, or know about it. And in the end, I wear this new persona (you know, the one trying so hard to look like he has his act together) like a secondhand suit, and I carry myself self-consciously.

At one time I believed in grace—but now I have seen it. It wasn't where I expected to find it. I have found grace where I found God, and I found God in the pressure points of life. The grace appeared in my brokenness, messiness, and confusion. I have surrendered to grace when I'm able to say that if I never did one more seminar or wrote one more book or attended one more meeting, it would be okay.

And when I understand this about grace and God, I am free to surrender, free to stop compensating, and free to let my life heal, not by denying the pain, but by acknowledging it and keeping my heart open.

When I surrender to grace, I can give up my various sorts of damage control. I am free to own my life—this life, not some tidy imaginary life.

Inspirations

When I come in that door, I'm covered with blood sometimes, and they hug me. They love me, they take care of me, they treat me as a real human being. And then they feed me, and they massage me, and they give me adjustments. These are my people. This is my place. This is where I come to be with God.

—Quote in museum exhibit at St. Paul's, from a New York firefighter, about the volunteers who worked tirelessly in St. Paul's chapel. St. Paul's is the place— adjacent to the World Trade Center—where firefighters and rescue workers ate and slept in the days and weeks that followed the 9/11 tragedy at the World Trade Center. www.saintpaulschapel.org

A Powerful Pause for the Days Ahead

Identify one way you try to do damage control. Tell a friend about it so the two of you can encourage each other. What does it mean to **let go** in order to receive grace?

20

For Easter: Home

Our true home is in the present moment. . . . The miracle is not to walk on water. The miracle is to walk on the green Earth in the present moment. . . . Peace is all around us—in the world and in nature—and within us—in our bodies and our spirits.

—THICH NHAT HANH, *TOUCHING PEACE*

Early in the movie *Blood Diamond*, a Mende village is plundered by a group of Revolutionary United Front (RUF) rebels. Many people, including women and children, are murdered. The young boys of the village are taken, to be trained to fight with the rebels. This group includes Dia, son of fisherman Solomon Vandy. Solomon's life is spared, but he is separated from his family and is enslaved to work in the diamond fields under the command of Captain Poison.

Eventually, Solomon finds his son. But Dia refuses to acknowledge him because he's been brainwashed by the rebels. Dia points a gun at Solomon's head. But Solomon begins to talk to Dia: "Dia, what are you doing? Dia! Look at me, look at me. What are you doing? You are Dia Vandy, of the proud Mende tribe. You are a good boy who loves soccer and school. Your mother loves you so much. She waits by the fire making plantains, and red palm oil stew with your sister N'Yanda and the new baby. The cows wait for you. And Babu, the wild dog who minds no one but you. I know they made you do bad things, but you are not a bad boy. I am your father who loves you. And you will come home with me and be my son again."

With tears streaking his young face, Dia lowers his gun and falls into his father's embrace. He is home.

There are many things that take us away from home: anger, busyness, self-importance, vengeance, unforgiveness, despair, frenzied consumerism, and heartache. The leaving is seldom sudden. But in every instance there is this reality: this new weight becomes the definition for our identity. It tells us who we are. And it requires that we focus on the peripheral issues, on the many things, on whatever is needed to impress or manipulate or use or perform.

Like Dia, we cannot undo these "bad things." But we can allow ourselves to fall into the embrace of Grace. That falling allows us to be truly at home, all right inside our own skin, and fully alive to the present moment.

Inspirations

But while he was still a long way off, his father saw him and was filled with compassion for him; he ran to his son, threw his arms around him and kissed him.

—THE GOSPEL OF LUKE,
STORY OF THE PRODIGAL SON

A Powerful Pause for the Days Ahead

Do you have a place of rest where you are at home in your own skin? If possible, go there, even if only in your imagination.

PART FOUR

Late Spring

21

Dandelions

*If dandelions were rare and fragile, people would . . .
pay $24.95 a plant, raise them by hand in greenhouses,
and form dandelion societies and all that. But they are
everywhere and don't need us and kind of do what they
please. So we call them "WEEDS" and murder them
at every opportunity.*

—ROBERT FULGHUM, *ALL I REALLY NEED
TO KNOW I LEARNED IN KINDERGARTEN*

Behind my house is a large hole. It's going to be a pond. You know, someday.

For the first year, my son loved it. The mud pit.

The large hole behind my house was going to be a pond four years ago. Now it is a hole, full of dandelions. An amphitheater of dandelions. As if a five-gallon bucket of butter yellow paint were poured, creating a river to where the waterfall will begin, 140 feet away. All summer, a river of yellow. One visitor commented, "What a creative idea, make a river and pond of dandelions. I never would have thought of that. It's beautiful."

"Yes," I said, "I planned it this way." What I saw as blight or failure, they saw as genius. Go figure.

A couple of months ago I lectured in Spokane for the Inland Empire Gardeners Club. The subject they gave me: Learning to love our dandelions. I said something like this: "I had a lawn I prided myself on, and I was plagued with dandelions that I fought with every means in my power. So learning to love them was no easy matter. I began by talking to them each day. I was cordial, friendly. They maintained a sullen silence. They were smarting from the war I had waged against them and were suspicious of my motives. But it wasn't long before they smiled back. And relaxed. Soon we were good friends.

"My lawn, of course, was ruined. But, how attractive my new garden became."

As gardeners, and as people, we have to decide if we're going to manage life or live it. The thing about dandelions is that they feel like something unmanaged, unplanned, untidy, out of control. And we don't like untidy things, whether in our garden, on our desk, in our mind or our soul. We are compelled to fix it, resolve it, manage it, and make it tidy.

We gardener's know all about this syndrome. Go to any gardener's home, and the first words from his or her lips: "I'm sorry. You should have seen my garden last week. Or wait until next week. Or don't look there. Or wait until I finish that bed, it'll be spectacular."

There is a wonderful seduction in the promise of tomorrow's potential to fix or remake. But we pay a price by looking to a more orderly tomorrow (which never gets here anyway, you may have noticed). When we focus on what we'll fix or manage better, we end up withholding our passion, commitment, energy, attention, and hope from today's bed of flowers.

Here's a reason to really love dandelions: They invite us to a spirituality of imperfection. A spirituality of loving today as it comes to us, dandelions and all.

A Powerful Pause for the Days Ahead

What is, for you, a daily reminder (such as dandelions) that your life is not perfect? Consider saying a prayer of thanks for your dandelions.

22

Putting Down the Sack

Within you there is a stillness and sanctuary to which
you can retreat at any time and be yourself.
—HERMAN HESSE, *SIDDHARTHA*

The traveler carries a large sack. He stops for a moment, stooped by its heaviness.

A passerby asks, "What's in your sack?"

"My mother."

"Isn't she heavy?"

"She sure is."

"Why don't you put her down?"

"I can't."

"Well, why can't you stop carrying her?"

"I don't know. I've always carried her."

I know this: I, too, carry a sack and am reluctant to set it down.

What is in the sack is not the primary issue.

Our sacks can carry a whole lot of things:

the anxiety of the day
past grievances
woundedness
an unfair life
a preoccupation with busyness
our desire for perfection
self-righteousness
our need to impress

Whatever it is, we find reassurance in the weight. Whatever it is, every single one prevents us from accepting life today as a gift.

I am traveling from New York to Dallas. Next to me, a young man, thirtyish, works at his laptop. Until the plane takes off, he is conducting business on his cell phone. On his armrest table are reports and other paperwork. He is dressed in his business attire, a perfectly starched shirt, tie still knotted. His dress and his focus impress me. I am reading a novel. During the meal, he asks, "So, what do you do?"

My usual response to that inquiry is, "I'm a TV evangelist," mostly because people do a double take, and for the rest of the flight are likely to leave me undisturbed.

"I'm a writer."

"Like Stephen King?"

"Very similar," I say.

Then I tell him about my book *Soul Gardening*. And he proceeds to tell me a story.

"When I was a boy in northern Texas, my grandmother had a garden. And she loved green beans. And she loved me. One of my favorite memories is helping my grandmother pick green beans. Today, my life is good. I have a big house and a bigger mortgage. But that means that I work sixty-hour weeks, and I have a hard time keeping up my commitments to my wife and three kids. And sometimes I get a little overwhelmed. I've never told anyone this, but last year I planted a green bean plant in back of my house. It's not much, and it made my wife laugh, but it's amazing what it does to my blood pressure every time I return home from a trip. It reminds me of my grandmother. Peaceful somehow. Strange, huh?"

No, I tell him, not strange at all.

When he visits his green bean plant, he sets down his sack. When he visits his green bean plant, he practices sanctuary. A sanctuary is a place where a person is at home with his own company. It is a place of rest, a powerful pause.

Everybody needs a green bean plant. Because, in our hurried and overhyped world, we need sanctuaries.

This is a simple truth. Just not so simple to follow through on.

My sanctuary is my garden. Unfortunately, I have been away from home for a few days, so my schedule is off-kilter. I miss my garden. Parts of my trip did not go as planned, so I'm out of whack. Anxious. I am eager to return to my sanctuary.

But perhaps Hesse is right: that sanctuary can be within us, too. What if I can't get to my garden for days? What if you can't go to your sanctuary when you need it most? We may have our physical locations—beside green bean plants or on garden paths—but we really can go inside to lay down the sack and find sanctuary.

I have spent the last few days in the Ottawa National Forest in the Upper Peninsula of Michigan. My father lives in a small town up here, in the middle of nowhere. Even MapQuest asks, Are you sure this is your destination?

Yesterday I followed a four-wheeler track trough the forest. Somewhere along the way, a bear scented me before I saw him; but I followed his tracks for a good while, hoping (against better judgment) for a chance encounter. No luck. But I did stop to rest—fortunately near a patch of wild blueberries. I filled my mouth with sweet berries and let the sun warm my face. There was no sound, save a breeze rustling the birch leaves. I took a breath and set down my sack.

~~~~~~~~~~~~~~~~~~~~~~~~~~~~~~~~~~~~

A Powerful Pause for the Days Ahead

Visit a garden. Give yourself time to wander and breathe in the sense of sanctuary. You can take this sense home with you and allow it to fill your sanctuary within.

> ~~~ **Visit** www.quietgarden.co.uk to find a garden near you that is dedicated to providing sanctuary.

23

What We Want to See

*It has been the interruptions to everyday life which
have most revealed the divine mystery of which I am
a part, all these interruptions presented themselves as
opportunities to go beyond the normal patterns of daily
life and find deeper connections than the previous safety
of my physical, emotional and spiritual well being.*

—HENRI NOUWEN, *BEYOND THE MIRROR*,

ADAPTED

A man discovered his brand new set of golf clubs had been
stolen from his garage. He had a suspect in mind. A teenage boy next door seemed the most likely candidate.

Sleuthlike, the man began watching the boy's comings and
goings, and what he saw only confirmed his suspicions. The boy
carried the air of a thief.

The boy walked, shoulders hunched, like a thief. He talked
nervously, like a guilty person would talk. His eyes darted like
a thief's eyes would.

After two weeks of watching, the man was certain that the
boy had stolen the golf clubs.

One afternoon, the man answered his phone. His brother-in-law said, cheerfully, "Hey buddy, I forgot to tell you. I borrowed your golf clubs the other day. Do you need them back?"

The next morning, the man watched as the boy left the house. And the man noticed an extraordinary thing: he no longer walked like a thief.

I've had another complicated week—a full and busy week. I have been traveling, so I miss my garden and its sanctuary and Sabbath space.

Add to that the weather here in Baltimore, where I am doing the Gardens and Grace Conference. We've had a nor'easter, which in translation means: Do you own a boat? Is your middle name Noah? A nor'easter is relentless rain—double-your-meds kind of rain.

I can feel my mood sour, and my time shrink. And I look at my circumstances in the exact same way that the man looked at the young neighbor. I see the circumstances as interruptions, which (like thieves) are squeezing out the Sabbath, the sanctuary, and any sense of calm from my life. Yes, it is clear that these circumstances are in fact stealing my life.

I saw in these circumstances what I wanted to see. What I needed to see. I see this happen in my travel, when unforeseeable circumstances or events alter the way I planned to go about my day. And I pout or scream or feel put out. As if the circumstances of life are required to revolve around me. And when I do that, I miss what is present. And I miss any opportunity to see God (or the sacred) hidden there.

Etty Hillesum—a young Jewish woman who died in Auschwitz—called her diary *An Interrupted Life*. Addressing this question about our need for security, she writes, "There is a really deep well inside me. And in it dwells God. Sometimes I am there, too. But more often stones and grit block the well and God is buried beneath. Then He must be dug out again."

Still in a foul mood, I walked with a friend down a Baltimore city street, looking for a restaurant where we could finally have lunch. Seeking refuge from the deluge of rain, we ducked into a courtyard. Beyond its black iron gate, we stood in a space crammed and swollen with lush-leaved potted plants. I smiled and knew we had found a secret garden.

We sat by the garden window and savored our food, the conversation, and the gifts of the colors, textures, and flowers from the garden outside. In time, my perception of this day as my adversary gave way to an openness to receive a gift of grace from these unlikely circumstances. Apparently, the day and its untidy details were not thieves after all.

A Powerful Pause for the Days Ahead

At the end of the day, look back over its events and circumstances and recall where you noticed that the sacred was present. You might try doing this for several days in a row.

~~~ **Find** a sacred space in your day by visiting www.sacredspace.ie

24

Enough

He who knows he has enough is rich.

—LAO TZU, *TAO TE CHING*

You may recall that in *Mr. Rogers' Neighborhood*, Lady Elaine Fairchilde was the mischief maker. Lady Elaine was not a pretty puppet. To be fair, well, let us just say she was particularly beauty challenged.

In one particular episode, Lady Elaine was asked what she wanted to be when she grew up. She said without hesitation, "I want to be a princess."

They asked, "Oh. What will you do?"

"I'll bring all my friends over and they can tell me how pretty I am."

They asked, "Then what will you do?"

She said, "I'll say thank you."

"Then what will you do?"

She thought, "Hmmm. I'll have to get more friends and bring them in to tell me how pretty I am."

"Then what?"

"I'll say thank you."

"Then what?"

"I'll guess I'll have to get more friends and bring them in to tell me how pretty I am."

At some point in life we learn that there are never enough people to tell us how pretty we are (or how thin, or how famous, or how successful, or how indispensable). With our relentless pursuit of affirmation, we end up forfeiting our identity to the whims of public opinion.

This is no surprise in a world that bombards us with the requirement for *more*. I tried to buy a new phone the other day. I was offered the latest model that would allow me to watch movies on my phone. I asked, "Do you have a model that just takes phone calls?" His response: "Why would you want just that?"

The system is rigged to confirm that more is never enough.

While there is something about these additions (whatever is newer, faster, more improved, or in vogue) that appear to take care of something or fill a need, here's what I know: The pull and tug serve to separate me from the present. From this moment. From myself.

In his book *Front Porch Tales*, Philip Gulley wrote a childhood memory about his family's house. The house they fell in love with was red. Red was not a typical color back in the day. He remembers the Realtor suggesting that they paint the house a pleasant neutral color, so it would be easier to sell when they moved.

Gulley muses, "We hadn't even moved in, and we're being told how to sell the house."

Where is this place where we can be at home without needing something else? Without needing to paint things a different color—or bring in more friends to tell us how pretty we are?

God rested, not because he was tired. God rested to celebrate, to savor, to delight in, to play, to revel in the creation, to say, "It is good." God rested and declared it holy. In that rest, God is affirming that there is nothing to prove. We are invited to enter that rest. Sabbath is the invitation to rest from the tyranny of pursuit. From that rest, we can live, work, and relate out of acceptance rather than do those things for the sake of acceptance. This is enough.

Outside my study window on this May afternoon, birds gather at our feeder: goldfinch, purple finch, nuthatch, towhee, and thrush. Below, our cats sit, helpless and hopeful. On the pond a Mallard pair drifts, still indifferent to our invitation that they build their home here. The first rose to bloom in my garden this year, "Penelope," is apricot tinted and smells of cloves. The Japanese maple is bowed from last night's rain, and the droplets on the leaves glisten in the morning sun. It is enough. Zach is waiting (not so patiently) for me to finish this writing so that we can begin the third inning of our game of baseball.

Inspirations

Come to me, all you who are weary and burdened, and I will give you rest. Take my yoke upon you and learn from me, for I am gentle and humble in heart, and you will find rest for your souls. For my yoke is easy and my burden is light.

—JESUS, THE GOSPEL OF MATTHEW

A Powerful Pause for the Days Ahead

Write yourself a letter: These are the things I have loved in life. . . . These are the things I have tasted, have looked at, have smelled, have touched. . . .

25

Kindness

Three things in human life are important. The first is to be kind. The second is to be kind. And the third is to be kind.

—HENRY JAMES, QUOTED IN *HENRY JAMES: A LIFE*, BY LEON EDEL

Yesterday I revisited an old *Life* magazine photo: Two little girls looking no more than seven years old. They have pigtails, and their expressions are uncertain. They walk through a gauntlet of people. The girls are African American; the people in the crowd are white. In this black-and-white photo, the contrast is stark. The white faces are strained, twisted, and raging, caught by the camera as they scream epithets. In this photo, the crowd's anger appears a caricature, exaggerated for affect. Staring at it, I feel a chill.

I want to turn away from such ugliness in the human spirit. I want to say that this has nothing to do with me, with my world. I want to say that this is the behavior of only bad, evil, or crazy people.

There is a story that the microphones connected to the TV cameras recording this event, caught a conversation between the little girls. One says to the other, "Don't worry. Momma said if we're nice to them, they'd be nice to us."

I see these faces in that crowd, and I wonder. Have I ever shared their anger?

Some time back, I designed a garden for a man who had a prickly personality. At times he could be charming and engaging. But there were other times when he was petty, spiteful, even mean. The hardest part was knowing which of his personalities would be present in a given encounter. During his volatile moments, he would yell and be dismissive. I found it easy to dislike him, and for the most part, be dismissive in my own way. He became, in my mind, recalcitrant and unredeemable. Inwardly, I called him Mr. Despicable.

One day he expressed gratitude for a particular area of the garden, a place in which he was able to relax. "Thank you," he said, voicing the first kind words I'd heard from him. And suddenly I saw beyond his bluster, beyond that steely and unpleasant exterior. I realized that somewhere inside was a frightened boy who didn't quite know how to escape this emotional fort he'd been hiding behind.

And I wondered how my own labeling had helped him continue to hide. Because as long as he acted as I had labeled him, and as long as I treated him according to that label, I intentionally withheld any kindness, opting to nurse my resentment. We were caught up in the same act, and it hurt both of us.

So I remind myself to be kind today. Even to Mr. Despicable.

And I think of the young girls. And I hear their sincere and profound courage, and I wonder, where does such courage come from? Is it in all of us?

The only way I can be kind to you is to be present to you, and the only way to be present to you is to pause.

Inspirations

In everything do to others as you would have them do to you.

—JESUS, THE GOSPEL OF MATTHEW

~~~~~~~~~~~~~~~~~~~~~~~~~~~~~~~

A Powerful Pause for the Days Ahead

Sit still for a while with the idea of kindness. What images and words come to mind?

26

Five More Minutes

Nothing can be more useful to a man than a determination not to be hurried.

Henry David Thoreau, journal entry
March 22, 1842

At a playground, a woman sits down next to a man on a park bench. "That's my son over there," she tells him, pointing to a little boy in a red sweater, gliding down the slide.

"He's a fine-looking boy," the man said. "That's my son on the swing in the blue sweatshirt." Then, looking at his watch, he calls, "What do you say we go, Todd?"

Todd pleads, "Dad, just five more minutes. Please? Just five more minutes."

The man nods, and Todd continues swinging, looking elated. Many minutes pass, and the father calls again, "Todd, what do you think? Time to go now?"

"Five more minutes, Dad. Just five more minutes." The man smiles and says, "Okay."

"My," the woman says, "you certainly are a patient father."

The man smiles. "Last year, my older son, Tommy, was killed by a drunk driver while he was riding his bike, not far from here. I never spent much time with Tommy. And now, I'd give anything for just five more minutes with him. So I've vowed not to make the same mistake with Todd. He thinks he has five more minutes to swing. But the truth really is, I get five more minutes to watch him play."

Last week, I led a memorial service for a friend who, in his early fifties, died too young. So we gathered together and we celebrated, told stories (some happy, some sad), shared memories, and, as one might expect, even nursed a little lament. As one friend put it in his eulogy, "I'm sitting here thinking, I sure wish I had called him every time I had the urge."

I understand. It is easy to second-guess, or to fear dying an unlived life, or to castigate ourselves for wasted moments.

But here's the deal: well-intentioned or not, nursed regret only puts more padding between me and the present moment, which includes the people and choices that are in my life today.

Life is about the choices we make now, with these five more minutes.

Jesus' counsel, three little words: "Do not worry."

I like the take of this eighty-three-year-old woman, in this quote sent in by a reader: "I'm not saving anything; I use my good china and crystal for every special event such as losing a pound, getting the sink unstopped, or the first amaryllis blossom. I wear my good blazer to the market. My theory is, if I look prosperous, I can shell out $28.49 for one small bag of groceries. I'm not saving my good perfume for special parties, but wearing it for clerks in the hardware store and tellers at the bank. 'Someday' and 'one of these days' are losing their grip on my vocabulary."

My good friend knows wine. Writes about it, appreciates it, savors it. He also knows wine people—folks who have grand and exceptional wine cellars. He told me the story of a couple with one such cellar, a collection to admire. Now mature in age, the couple knew that their years were numbered, and that many of their friends had died with full wine cellars, those rare bottles collected for a special occasion. "You know," the gentleman told my friend, "we say we'll drink it when the occasion is right. And, for some reason, the occasion is never quite right." So they made a decision. They would collect no more wine. They would take delight in and share the wine that they have. In their words, they decided to "drink their cellar."

After he told me that story, I knew it was time to take my own medicine. I own a bottle of 1982 port. The really good stuff. After the first sip, this kind of port makes you say, out loud to the sky, "Now I know why God created grapes." But I've been keeping the bottle for the right event. What kind of event will it take?

This morning, early, with coffee in hand, I walked the garden alone (if we don't count Bernie, one of our tabby cats who moseyed along). I stopped often, savored a few things that I missed yesterday. And enjoyed a good hit of gooseflesh from the delphiniums, in their stately, extravagant, ephemeral, and wasteful splendor. I'm going in for breakfast soon. Really. In five more minutes.

Inspirations

Therefore do not worry about tomorrow, for tomorrow will worry about itself. Each day has enough troubles of its own.

—JESUS, THE GOSPEL OF MATTHEW

A Powerful Pause for the Days Ahead

Treat yourself to something you enjoy—a good cup of coffee, a bowl of ice cream, a certain path you like to walk, a flower whose fragrance you love. And spend five more minutes enjoying that joy.

PART FIVE

Early Summer

27

Broken Glass

This isn't where I expected to be. My version of myself,
my life didn't have this.

—RAM DASS, AFTER HIS STROKE, IN
DOCUMENTARY *RAM DASS: FIERCE GRACE*

The Rev. John Young-Jung Lee gives a vivid description of a scene near the end of Leonard Bernstein's 1971 musical work entitled *Mass.*

There is a scene in which the priest is richly dressed in magnificent vestments. He is lifted up by the crowd carrying a splendid glass chalice in his hands. Suddenly the human pyramid collapses and the priest comes tumbling down. His vestments are ripped off and the glass chalice falls to the ground, shattering into tiny pieces.

As he walks slowly through the debris of his former glory, barefoot and wearing only a T-shirt and jeans, he hears children's voices singing off stage, Laude. Laude. Laude. Praise! Praise! Praise! His eyes, transformed by God's grace, suddenly notice the broken chalice. He looks at it for a long, long time. And then, haltingly, he says, "I never realized that broken glass could shine so brightly." (www.dpuc.org/sermon080413.htm)

Things do not always go the way we plan. Not that we don't try to make them work. Somehow, well-made plans make us feel better, more presentable, even acceptable.

But things change. Life turns left. Plans, dreams, relationships break and shatter. Hearts get broken.

When this happens to me, I want it all to go away. And truth be told, sometimes I deal with my own fear of brokenness by trying my darnedest to fix other people.

I spent some time with a group of people weighed down by broken things. They invited me to sit, to listen, and, if I had any, to offer some insight.

I wanted to say all the right things. I wanted, in effect, to fix it. I wanted to put the chalice back together.

But since when are tidiness and the presence of the sacred one in the same?

In the end, I realized that all I could do was invite them to the epiphany of the priest in Bernstein's *Mass*. If we have eyes to see, there are no unsacred moments. And God is alive and well in all things.

Even in our broken glass.

Inspirations

God is near to the brokenhearted.

—PSALM 34

～～～～～～～～～～～～～～～～～～～～～～～

A Powerful Pause for the Days Ahead

Think about a failure. What did it feel like? What did you learn? Why are we so afraid of failure?

28

Time Management

The moment one gives close attention to anything, even a blade of grass, it becomes a mysterious, awesome, indescribably magnificent world in itself.

—HENRY MILLER, ATTRIBUTED

I need to get an essay written. But before I begin to put thoughts on the page, I decide to finish my coffee and go through the mail. I receive a brochure advertising a workshop. (I do read all my junk mail. It makes me feel wanted.) The brochure promises that the workshop "will change the way I see the world." Now there's a guarantee worth considering. The good-hearted people leading the workshop want me to lead a meaningful life (I can't argue with that), and the brochure tells me that I can lead a meaningful life if I "practice time management." For three hundred dollars, I can spend a day at a time-management workshop.

The brochure tells me that fewer than one in five people begin the day with a plan. Which makes me wonder about my own plan for this day, and I can't come up with one.

But I have an excuse. There's a wagonload of stuff swirling around my head that's begging to be worried about. Did you know, for example, that this month, July, is Bioterrorism/Disaster Education Month? It is also Cell Phone Courtesy Month. And National Blueberry Month. National Hot Dog Month. National Recreation and Parks Month. And Social Wellness Month. Apparently, this is the month set aside for us to improve social and communication skills and learn how to act properly to create a positive and lasting first impression. However, since I didn't have a plan, I haven't been able to decide which cause to focus on.

The truth is, today I'm in no mood to give any energy to bioterrorism education. But the blueberries get me thinking about an ice cream sundae. So I go to town with my family. It is our Island Festival weekend. We sit on the lawn in Ober Park and listen to Bob's Your Uncle. This is one of our homegrown bands (all teachers during the day, banjo and mandolin and guitar pickers by weekend or night). Zach and his friends roll down the grassy hills. I'm lost in the music, until I remember that I still don't have a plan for the day. So, during a break, I walk to the local pizza parlor for something to eat, something to give me the energy to think and concoct a plan.

"I have your book," the pizza parlor owner tells me. "My mother-in-law, in California, called me and said, 'You've got to read this book.' So she sent me a copy, and I looked on the back and saw your picture and said, 'Oh my god, I know him.'"

"Thank you," I say, not sure if this is a compliment, "I'll have a pizza and a beer."

"I like the fact that you can read it in little parts," she tells me enthusiastically.

"Yes," her husband adds, "I think it's the perfect bathroom book."

Oh my Lord. I have to tell you that some compliments truly bring tears to the eyes. This is one of those moments.

"Thank you," I say. "Better make that two beers."

Where was I? Oh yes, the need to have a plan for my day.

But now I'm thinking, why do I need a plan if I have already written the perfect bathroom book? (I can't wait until my publisher begins to use this fact in future advertising.)

Walking back to the park, I get worried, thinking about that brochure. So where does my day—this day—stack up? You know, as a building block to a meaningful life? Without a plan, I've already conceded that I am a disappointment to the folks leading the seminar. But you've got to admit, we live in a culture with very odd measurements for success—all of it meted out in the slings and arrows of advertising. Just last week I stood in a bookstore, in front of a section named "success library." A whole lot of books guaranteed to give me a meaningful life. Next to it, you guessed it, was the "financial library." (It is not, I was sad to see, next to the "great bathroom book" section.)

You can't help but walk away from those shelves thinking, *If only I could digest one of those books, my life would be better.* And it hits me, on the way back to the park, how much mental energy goes into navigating this bombardment. And how little mental energy is left for sitting still, for listening, for giving, for making music, for sharing, for savoring the moment, for laughing with friends.

To be honest, I have nothing against time management. There's something to be said for not giving in to the urgent at the expense of the important. I know a lot of people who have their schedule, calendar, and BlackBerry ducks in a row, beginning each day with a plan and a list, but that doesn't mean that they are paying attention. Or that they are present. It just might mean that they're *extremely* tidy people. And I'm not so sure that's a good career goal.

All this hyperactivity brings to mind the old story about an exhausted woodcutter who kept wasting time and energy chopping wood with a blunt ax because he did not have the time, he said, to stop and sharpen the blade.

It's late afternoon. Truth be told, I still don't have a plan.

I'm a sucker for these junk-mail brochures, because whatever our life is like, on many days we wish it were different. But I'm not so sure that a seminar will make the difference. According to a lot of these seminar people, my life as it is will never be enough. But it seems enough to me to be here with my family and listen to Bob's Your Uncle and eat my bacon and garlic pizza while my son rolls down the hill with his friends.

As far as changing the way I see the world? Well, I'll go with the wisdom of Jesus, who said, "What shall it profit a man if he gains the whole world but loses his soul." Buddha had it right, "If we could see the miracle of a single flower clearly, our whole life would change."

Not long ago, a man stood to give the eulogy at his father's funeral. "What I remember about my dad," he told those gathered, "is that he never finished anything. He always had projects he started. And projects he never finished. I used to think he lacked gumption or motivation. But now I see it differently. My dad never finished those projects because he used that time for something else. He spent that time with us. His children. When we needed him or his time, he was always there. Now, I see it."

Our day is over, and Zach is ready for bed. I stick my head in the door of his bedroom to say good night.

"Dad," he says to me, "next time you take a bath, try Celtic bagpipe music. It is soooo relaxing. Really Dad, it is soooo relaxing."

I smile. I can't hide my laugh.

My young son gets it. And he never attended the seminar. I guess there's no need to ask him what his plan was for the day.

Now that I think of it, I do have a plan. I am going to pay attention.

Inspirations

What shall it profit a man if he gains the whole world but loses his soul?

—Jesus, the Gospel of Matthew

~~~~~~~~~~~~~~~~~~~~~~~~~~~~~~~

A Powerful Pause for the Days Ahead

This week, make a point to get away from your time-management tools for a day. Spend that day paying attention to the people and other wonders in your life.

29

It's the Little Things

I once spoke to my friend, an old squirrel, about the
Sacraments—
he got so excited
and ran into a hollow in his tree and came
back holding some acorns, an owl feather,
and a ribbon he had found.
And I just smiled and said, "Yes, dear,
you understand:
everything imparts
His grace.

—St. Francis of Assisi, adapted from
his writings by Daniel Ladinsky in
Love Poems from God

Here's your assignment," I instructed the group of educators at a recent retreat. "Take a walk—a specific walk. Walk to the harbor park. Walk to the government building. I want you to walk to that destination as fast as you can, with eyes straight ahead. Focus only on your destination.

119

"After you arrive, stop, catch your breath. Then I want you to return here by walking (sauntering, loitering, ambling, meandering) *slowly*. If you took five minutes to get there, take fifteen minutes to return. This time, notice things. Pay attention to your senses. What do you see, smell, hear, even taste?"

The responses were surprising. People talked about colors. Sounds. Conversations. Images. Specific pictures.

Here's the instructive part. What did people notice? All the little things. The little things that are a blur when we are moving too fast. At another recent retreat, I had the participants collect items for a "sacrament box." Among the items in the box were a heart-shaped stone, the exoskeleton of a dragonfly, the spiny nut from a sweet gum tree, and a cobalt-blue flower of a morning glory.

This is what we mean by the phrase, "finding God in all things."

Even the little things. Have you ever looked at the flower of the hardy geranium, or *Geranium x magnificum*, up close, with a magnifying glass? I have. The color is deep, regal lavender. Running from the center are veins in a deeper tone, like bruised purple. Close-up they look raised, ridgelines on petals of ephemeral paper. I am absorbed. And enthralled.

In Christian vocabulary, *Sacrament* means a "sign of grace."

Every time we give in to a culture that ratchets up the noise about whatever is bigger or faster or newer, we worship at the altar of the superlative. As a result, we miss all the good stuff; we walk right by it every day. We don't see the little miracles, those astonishing signs of grace.

Inspirations

Consider the lilies of the field.

—JESUS, THE GOSPEL OF MATTHEW

~~~~~~~~~~~~~~~~~~~~~~~~~~~~~~~~~~~~~~~

A Powerful Pause for the Days Ahead

Take your own walk to a specific location. Go fast to get there but slow way down when you return. And notice things. Ponder. Partake of these everyday sacraments.

~~~ **Need** help slowing down in the midst of your hectic days? Sign up for the 3-Minute Retreat at www.loyolapress.com/retreat and receive a daily email reminding you to pause for three minutes of simple meditation each day.

30

Losing What I Don't Need

Without solitude of some sort, there is and can be no
maturity. Unless one becomes empty and alone, he can-
not give himself in love, because he does not possess the
deep self which is the only gift worthy of love.

—THOMAS MERTON, *DISPUTED QUESTIONS*

There's a story that Socrates saw a heap of gold and jewelry being carried through the streets of Athens. Upon seeing it he exclaimed, "Look how many things there are which I don't need or want." Impressive. Imagine him walking through Costco!

Here is what I find interesting: we assume that something outside of ourselves will improve our lot in life. This notion caused Pascal to suggest (a long time ago), "If our condition were truly happy, we would not need diversion from it in order to make ourselves happy."

Advertisements fuel the fire, no doubt. I just saw the new statistic that to be truly happy in retirement, it would be good to have $5 million set aside. Okay. How much will I need to save to be mildly unperturbed?

Blame it on age, but I tend to lose a lot of stuff. Misplace. Forget. And every time, it unnerves me. I forget things when I pack for my travels: my lecture notes, a tie, a shirt, or my socks. Thank God for e-tickets and cell phones with memory dial.

On my recent trip, I left a sweatshirt on the plane. The week before, I lost my glasses, my favorite glasses—the ones that made me look young, handsome, and desirable. On this last trip, I lost my favorite fountain pen. That one got me. I've been writing with that pen for fifteen years. It knows me, has bled for me.

Yesterday, I lost my cell phone. After looking for an hour, I found it, hooked onto my back jeans pocket.

What is it about losing stuff, ordinary stuff, that exasperates and depletes us?

There is something about the significance we attach to stuff. I just finished Alain de Botton's fine book, *Status Anxiety*, about what happens when we need to keep up with someone, or something, or some perception about the way life should be. Always something just beyond our grasp.

Reading de Botton made me think. We collect stuff: accouterments, titles, opinions, belief systems, toys, and retirement funds. Somehow, we need this stuff to be somebody.

Don Shula, famous former coach of the Miami Dolphins, was vacationing with his family in a small northeastern town—a one-cinema town. The family wanted to go to the afternoon matinee. With tickets in hand, they entered the theater. A young man near the back stood, faced Shula, and applauded and cheered and shouted.

Shula was taken aback, but duly impressed. He approached the young man and shook his hand. "Thank you," he said. "Not many people recognize me up here, and not many are as effusive in their appreciation."

The young man said, "Sir, I don't know you from Adam. But the theater owner said he would not show the movie unless there were ten people. And you are number ten."

Who are we without our stuff?

I had a bad day; some phone calls shook me, making me wonder about my own sufficiency and value. Now I'm on my deck, nursing a little self-pity. The sun is on my face, the sound of the nearby stream lulls me. One of our cats is in deep slumber under my chair, and our son, Zach, plays on the lawn. The canna lilies in the pot near my chair are a deep blood red.

But even here, in my anxiety, I need something. I've lost something, something much more important than my glasses or cell phone. I've lost the sense that I'm enough without all my stuff—the praise, the success, even the satisfied feeling at a job well done.

And in the breeze, I hear one word: Terry. The Spirit is saying my name, and by doing that he affirms that everything I seek is already here, right inside me.

I don't know if there is a patron saint for this kind of afternoon. But I say a prayer nonetheless.

Inspirations

Our deepest fear is not that we are inadequate. Our deepest fear is that we are powerful beyond measure. It is our light, not our darkness that most frightens us. We ask ourselves, Who am I to be brilliant, gorgeous, talented, fabulous? Actually, who are you not to be? You are a child of God. Your playing small does not serve the world. There is nothing enlightened about shrinking so that other people won't feel insecure around you. We are all meant to shine, as children do. We were born to make manifest the glory of God that is within us. It's not just in some of us; it's in everyone. And as we let our own light shine, we unconsciously give other people permission to do the same. As we are liberated from our own fear, our presence automatically liberates others.

—MARIANNE WILLIAMSON,
A RETURN TO LOVE

A Powerful Pause for the Days Ahead

In one small area of your home, gather up the stuff you don't use. Put it away or give it away.

~~~ **Donate** clothes and other items you don't use: www.goodwill.org or www.salvationarmyusa.org, or www.svdpusa.org.

31

Big Swords

We are an incarnate word, spoken by God, still being spoken by God, a word of grace, of reconciliation, truth, love, healing. But our word is often garbled. Part of our struggle here is to liberate the word within us so that it can be spoken clearly.

—ROBERT MULHOLLAND,
SHAPED BY THE WORD

Once upon a time, Mister Rogers went into battle against a little boy with a big sword. It was a big plastic contraption with lights and sound effects, and it was the kind of sword used in defense of the universe by the heroes of the television shows that the little boy liked to watch. The little boy didn't watch Mr. Rogers's show, and so when Mister Rogers knelt down in front of him, the little boy with the big sword looked past him and through him.

Mister Rogers wasn't going anywhere. Yes, sure, he was taping, and right there, in Penn Station in New York City, were rings of other children wiggling in wait for him, but right now his patient gray eyes were fixed on the little boy with the big sword, and so he stayed there, on one knee, until the little boy's eyes finally focused on Mister Rogers, and the boy said, "It's a death ray."

The boy's mother said, "Do you want to give Mister Rogers a hug, honey?" But the boy was shaking his head no, and Mister Rogers was sneaking his face past the big sword and the armor of the little boy's eyes and whispering something in his ear—something that, while not changing his mind about the hug, made the little boy look at Mister Rogers in a new way, with the eyes of a child at last, and nod his head yes.

Later, one of the people with him asked what he'd said to the boy.

"Oh, I just knew that whenever you see a little boy carrying something like that, it means that he wants to show people that he's strong on the outside. I just wanted to let him know that he was strong on the inside, too. And so that's what I told him. I said, 'Do you know that you're strong on the inside, too?' Maybe it was something he needed to hear." (Adapted from Tom Junod's "Can you say . . . 'Hero'?" in *Esquire*, November 1998.)

I can relate. I know what it's like to not feel strong on the inside. I do know that I have a sword on the inside. And I know what it is like to take out my sword and do my best to impress everyone around me.

I do know that it's some sort of sleight of hand. If you see the sword, you won't notice the little boy in me.

I also know that life's pace just makes matters worse. Because a fast-paced life carries with it the need to look strong all the time.

We assume that our identity is predicated on consumption (more) and velocity (hurry). And our mantra becomes, "This is not enough"—"this" meaning relationship or job or circumstance or conversation or possession or whatever. Given my need to impress, consume, acquire, or rush, I end up sword fighting everything around me.

I need Mr. Rogers's reminder: There is a word spoken about me. It tells me that I am strong on the inside. And not because of anything I have done, or failed to do. It is the incarnate word, spoken by God. Robert Benson writes in *Between the Dreaming and the Coming True:* "The Hebrew word for it is *dabhar,* 'God spoke.' It is the word found in Genesis to describe the way the world came to be. God spoke the light. God spoke the Christ. God spoke Robert. God spoke Fred and Annie and Sara and Cindy and Alan and Barbara—and you too, whatever your name is."

God spoke Terry. A reminder not easy to hear in the noise, the bustle, and the velocity of life's competing voices.

God spoke. This is not just about self-esteem, and it's not about adding one more thing to life to make it strong enough or meaningful enough. When we remind ourselves that God spoke us—you and me, just as we are—we can rest in who we are. We can allow ourselves to be loved as who we are.

I need to ask myself often, *Are you willing to be loved for being this you?* If I answer yes, then I guess I don't need my sword today.

Inspirations

To be nobody but myself in a world which is doing its best night and day, to make you everybody else—means to fight the hardest battle which any human being can fight, and never stop fighting.

—EE CUMMINGS, QUOTED IN *LETTER TO A HIGH SCHOOL EDITOR*

~~~~~~

A Powerful Pause for the Days Ahead

Sit with this story. Put yourself in Zusia's place.

Once, the great Hassidic leader Zusia came to his followers. His eyes were red with tears, and his face was pale with fear. "Zusia, what's the matter?"

"The other day, I had a vision of the question that the angels will ask me about my life."

The followers were puzzled. "Zusia, you are pious. You are scholarly and humble. You have helped so many of us. What question about your life could be so terrifying that you would be frightened to answer it?"

Zusia turned his gaze to heaven. "I have learned that the angels will not ask me, 'Why weren't you a Moses, leading your people out of slavery?'"

His followers persisted. "So, what will they ask you?"

"They will say to me, 'Zusia, there was only one thing that no power of heaven or earth could have prevented you from becoming.' They will say, 'Zusia, Zusia, why were you not Zusia?'"

32

The Balanced Life

Having a good time. Wish I was here.

—*POSTCARDS FROM THE EDGE*

It happened again. I was going to get some writing done, but I received an email from my friend in Texas. She asks, "Okay . . . how do I keep balance? I am feeling overwhelmed by the book and a year or more of travel, signing, speaking engagements, 2 houses, 4 dogs, 3 B&B's, and a partridge in a pear tree, and not being 20 anymore, and on and on. I know you will know the answer."

I'm glad for the email, and I want to be helpful. More than that, I want to rise to the occasion. But I'm not legally allowed to prescribe medication, so I'm wracking my brain for something profound to tell her.

I take a break, and am sitting on the bench in front of Bob's Bakery with my son, Zach. (Bob's is our community's morning gathering spot.) We're having cinnamon twists. They are decadently yummy and make me forget my need to be useful. The bench is made from a trunk of an old downed log, its seat now worn from years of time and use. Zach and I watch the traffic—traffic in a poetic license sort of way—go by. And Zach, his mouth full of half a twist, says, "Dad, this is the life."

With every question about managing life, or finding balance, there is a knee-jerk temptation to offer solutions, which always means adding something else to the to-do list. In the end, it's like the book on ninety-nine ways to simplify my life because, apparently, one way is not enough. So it's relentless. I found another book about the "balance diet" (you know, getting my life in order), but after one week on the balance diet, I start to wonder how I'm doing, as if there's a test. And if I fail, am I required to attend a workshop on remedial balanced living? And I start to wonder about the benefit of the balanced life if I'm always looking over my shoulder to see who's impressed.

As if that isn't enough, we have a tendency to complicate the problem with our solutions, a superfluity of well-meaning activities to make our life worth living. In the words of T. S. Eliot, we are "distracted from distractions by distractions." I think of a pastor's conference I attended on "personal renewal." The conference agenda was crammed to the gills (6:00 a.m. to 10:00 p.m., I do not exaggerate), and at the end of the week we sat glassy-eyed and lifeless, hoping for some reprieve from this weight of good intentions.

And it starts early, doesn't it? I read this in the *New York Times*.

The word "kindergarten" means "children's garden," and for years has conjured up an image of children playing with blocks, splashing at water tables, dressing up in costumes or playing house. Now, with an increased emphasis on academic achievement even in the earliest grades, playtime in kindergarten is giving way to worksheets, math drills, and fill-in-the-bubble standardized tests. (Clara Hemphill, "On Education" July 26, 2006)

I saw another article about a neighborhood in Beverly Hills where it's against the association guidelines to build a house under 5,000 square feet. The houses average 10,000 to 40,000 square feet. I have no moral argument against building a big house, assuming that you are planning to house, say, an entire city block of families, or a small country.

The cultural gauntlet has been thrown down. Success is the goal. These people have "made it." Bigger is better. More is better. Faster is better. Somewhere, the real balance went out the window.

Mother Teresa apparently didn't get the memo. Think of it, she could have advertised the "fastest growing leper ministry."

I see it now. What Jesus needed was a spin doctor. Someone to talk with the press, to translate what he really meant when he said, "Blessed are the poor in spirit."

An organization recently asked me for my bio, and I'll admit that it gave me pause. I'd had a bad week. I was in a bookstore and saw my friend's book, which outsells mine 100 to 1. Which takes me back to standing in front of the "success library" in that same bookstore, asking, what is missing? This is all a very toxic and dangerous sort of stew, and can only be dispelled by looking at the way dusk settles on the rose

"Winchester Cathedral," outside my study window. As the petals absorb the light of dusk, all the other stuff that clutters my mind recedes. And I wonder, how do I put Zach's delight with a cinnamon twist on a resume?

If I can stop the noise, then the fragrance of the rose, the joy of my son, and the quickening of the morning air in the garden all tell me that I am living this life—or this moment, or this conversation, or this event—and no longer need to focus on what balance is or how to achieve it.

And if I did have an answer for my friend who asked how to keep in balance, the best I could say is, find a porch swing. This may not be the best answer in Texas right at the moment, since it's close to 150 degrees in the shade, but you get the idea.

Let's spend the afternoon on the porch. Let's crank up Van Morrison or Roy Orbison and let the afternoon heat recede into the trees. As the sun reaches the horizon, we watch and feel the earth itself breathe in relief. And the perfume from the lily "Casa Blanca" suffuses the air around the patio. We are absorbed in moments of grace. We find ourselves lost in what Rabbi Abraham Heschel calls "radical amazement."

Jesus didn't wait for things to reach a breaking point; he was proactive. He got up, and left—left the crowds and the accolades. He departed—to whatever served as a porch swing back then.

Was Jesus busy? Yes. Was Jesus in a hurry? Never. Now, if you ask me, that's balance.

Inspirations

Who can make muddy water clear? Let it be still, and it will gradually become clear of itself.

—Lao Tzu, *Tao Te Ching*

∼∼∼∼∼∼∼∼∼∼∼∼∼∼∼∼∼∼∼∼∼∼∼∼∼∼

A Powerful Pause for the Days Ahead

Today, if you have a porch swing, use it. If you don't have one, today's a good day to find one.

PART SIX

Late Summer

33

Holy Longing

The best beauty product is to have a life. A real life.
With challenges, disappointments, stress, and laughter.

—VERONIQUE VIENNE,

THE ART OF IMPERFECTION

Charlie Brown is standing at a candy counter. We don't see the salesperson behind the counter. We see only Charlie standing, with candy in hand, responding to her, "Yes, ma'am, I'd like to buy a box of valentine candy for a girl who doesn't know I exist."

"No ma'am," he says, "nothing too expensive."

He continues, "I'll never have the nerve to give it to her anyway."

I can relate to Charlie Brown. We are a mixture of longing and fear.

I know about longing. Longing is whatever the red-headed girl—the girl of Charlie's dreams—represents. It is the litany of "if onlys" and "what I've been waiting for," those objects of my longing that will offer me love, or contentment, or admiration, or affection, or well-being, or affirmation, or peace, or even just a day of rest.

We need—no, we require—something to gratify or satisfy the longing. In other words, the longing is a snag in the system; it's something that needs to be resolved. We tell ourselves that surely it is a sign of weakness, something that needs to be fixed.

Here's the tough question: am I willing to be loved for being me, standing at the counter with my bag of candy?

Because if I cannot, I will not be able to abide my disquiet.

Disquiet can feel like a weight we can't get rid of. We carry the weight of unrequited longing, of dreams that do not come true, of restless days in lives that are crammed full, of broken hearts and promises.

In this disquiet, I am really waiting for a life "not yet." And I am unable to embrace the life (even this longing-filled life) I have today. I miss the sacredness in all things—*all* things. I do not see that all of life, including my longings—those both realized and unrealized—are infused with the imprint of God.

And I know that maybe, just maybe, my longings themselves are holy, and I can rest in them. Even when I have a broken heart.

It's now Saturday night; I've finished my duties as guest speaker and retreat leader, and I enjoy a feast of catfish and blackberry cobbler at the Loco Coyote, a Texas hangout in the proverbial middle of nowhere. I will have to admit, that even though I say it is okay to abide my disquiet, catfish, hushpuppies, and cobbler come awfully close to satisfying whatever may have been nagging at me.

The sun has dipped beyond sight, and the horizon, stretched across an endless Texas sky, is a band of color, the deep orange of a ripe peach. Random steel blue clouds float above. The serenity calms me, and I feel at home, even with the parts of me that are still unresolved.

~~~~~~

A Powerful Pause for the Days Ahead

What do you desire? What are your unfulfilled longings? Don't edit this list! Ask God for the grace you need.

34

Rested Mules

There is more to life than merely increasing its speed.
—MOHANDAS GANDHI, ATTRIBUTED

A young minister returned to his hometown in northern Georgia. He struck up a conversation with an old farmer. They stood by the fencerow and watched as a new picking machine rolled through a cotton field. Until now, the farmer had picked cotton using a machine pulled by a team of mules.

"That's an amazing machine, picking six rows of cotton in minutes," the young man says in admiration.

"Yes it is," says the farmer, "but I've got to tell you, I really do miss my mules."

"Really? Why?"

"Because these machines work day and night, every day. My mules worked only six days a week, and then they needed a rest, so they had enough energy for the next week. When my mules rested, I rested. And I was better off for it."

In *Care of the Soul,* Thomas Moore writes that living artfully with time might only require something as simple as pausing. In our modern life—with its premium on speed, our internal governors set on *rush*—we have no time for reflection or pondering or for allowing impressions of the day to sink into our hearts.

We know that something is lost when we give up our mules. Our souls resonate with stillness, slowness, and renewal. We know that the mules represent something essential, even non-negotiable. Something restorative and grounding.

However, when speed is a priority, how do we go back?

Our conflict is made all the more difficult because the enticement of speed and instant information takes its toll unconsciously. Without realizing it, we give up our places of rest. "Flying home from Europe a few months ago," Mark Bittman, *New York Times* correspondent, writes, "I swiped a credit card through the slot of the in-seat phone, checked my e-mail and robbed myself of one of my two last sanctuaries." ("I Need a Virtual Break. No, Really," *New York Times,* March 2, 2008)

When we were building our current house on Vashon Island, Judith, Zach, and I lived in a rental house not far away from our new land. The house was old, with great character, and very comfortable—more than adequate for our eighteen-month stay. Oddly, after only a few weeks I became depressed. I felt lethargic and had no sense of motivation. After a few weeks it hit me. In this house, I had no garden. It was the first time in years that I lived in a house with no garden. For me, no garden means no sanctuary. No sanctuary means no place to pause and refuel.

More than ever, we need our mules.

When we do recognize the necessity of what the mules represent, we try to create the benefit with the very mindset that set the mules packing in the first place. John Dewey called it "compensatory maladjustments," or trying to make something right by overdoing or overexerting. I saw an ad for a Speed Bible, allowing one to read and understand it in only minutes. Hmm. Which is sort of like saying that we could stop and smell the roses, or, instead, just hang a rose air freshener from our rearview mirror (with the windows rolled up) while racing, because we're late for our next appointment.

I don't have any mules. But I do have a lot of birds that visit my pond. They invite me to pause. They are the benediction to my day.

I am on the back deck after dinner. It has been a full and busy day. And this pause is non-negotiable. It's bird bathing and feeding time. (Or, their equivalent of "Miller Time.") Some birds arrive in groups, others alone.

Tonight, a first for me: a Western Tanager—exotic in his distinctive red skull cap and yellow and black uniform, like a hockey-team jersey—bathes in the stream. Waiting for their turn, a family of Cedar Waxwings. Two males pose on the rocks nearby, stately and elegant, their feathers the tint of bone china. Lynyrd Skynyrd's "Free Bird" washes over me from the radio playing inside. This is heaven. Or very close to it.

Inspirations

Deep within us all there is an amazing inner sanctuary of the soul, a holy place, a Divine Center, a speaking Voice, to which we may continuously return.

—THOMAS R. KELLY,
A TESTAMENT OF DEVOTION

~~~~~~~~~~~~~~~~~~~~~~~~~~~~~~~~~~~

A Powerful Pause for the Days Ahead

What can serve as "mules" for you? Find something this week that helps you rest.

35

How Big Is Your Frying Pan?

We may ignore, but we can nowhere evade, the presence of God. The world is crowded with Him. He walks every-where incognito. And the incognito is not always hard to penetrate. The real labor is to remember, to attend. In fact, to come awake. Still more, to remain awake.

—C. S. Lewis, *Letters to Malcolm*

Standing in a pristine Alaskan stream, the fisherman pulls in his first catch, a lovely eighteen-inch trout. "Most impressive," his friend says, thinking of the delectable evening meal ahead. But the fisherman unceremoniously tosses the fish back into the stream.

He catches a second, then a third, each a bit larger than the last. But each beauty is tossed back into the stream.

The fourth catch is maybe six inches in length. This one the fisherman keeps for their evening supper.

His friend can't keep quiet any longer. "You catch three prize-winning trout and throw them back. You catch a runt and keep it. Why?"

"Because I only have an eight-inch frying pan."

At a recent retreat, one less-than-thrilled participant approached me at the end of the second day. The group had been talking about "embracing the sacred present" and "celebrating grace in the irreducible uniqueness of daily and ordinary existence." One project included collecting small articles of wonder (a leaf, a bird's feather, a misshapen stone, a piece of green glass), each a reminder to use in our final liturgy of celebration.

"This is not what I expected," the woman told me. "I assumed the retreat would be much more spiritual."

Laughing out loud seemed an unpastoral response, so I bit my tongue. I do know that her comment was more about her expectations than the experience itself.

And truth be told, I do the very same thing. I carry a frying pan that precludes my ability to see the many gifts (and surprises and wonders) of life. The size of our frying pan determines the way we see God. And *where* we see God.

As a young man I had a finely tuned theology of God. And I had certainty. This meant, unfortunately, that I relegated God to certain experiences—you know, the "more spiritual" ones. Every other experience, I threw back into the stream. As a result, my beliefs (suppositions and assumptions that were unquestioned and unchallenged) excluded the presence of the sacred from so much of my life.

Why? There is an odd sense of control in a one-size frying pan. We assume, wrongly, that we can orchestrate a spiritual encounter.

A young man, with plumber credentials in hand, stands at the railing to view Niagara Falls. "I think I can fix that," he said.

Also, we're stuck in our certainty.

A man lost his car keys. It was night, and he looked frantically near a street lamp. Someone walking by asked what was wrong.

"I've lost my keys," the man answered.

"Where?"

"Over there," he pointed.

"Well, if you lost them over there, why are you looking over here?"

"Because," he answered, "there's more light over here."

It turns out that the opposite of faith is not doubt but certainty. When we are certain, we lose our capacity for surprise.

I had a certain part of my life figured out. Fortunately, grace does not play by my rules. If, in fact, God walks everywhere incognito, it will mean that I have to learn how to celebrate a bawdy, unkempt spirit and an untidy, misunderstood God. This Spirit of love and transformation is present in everyone, doling out the extravagant gifts of that love and grace in kindness, service, healing, hope, and celebration.

Inspirations

Marvelous vision of the hills at 7:45 a.m. The same hills as always, as in the afternoon, but now catching the light in a totally new way, at once very earthly and very ethereal, with delicate cups of shadow and dark ripples and crinkles where I had never seen them, and the whole slightly veiled in mist so that it seemed to be a tropical shore, a newly discovered continent. And a voice in me seemed to be crying, "Look! Look!" For these are the discoveries, and it is for this that I am high on the mast of my ship (have always been), and I know that we are on the right course, for all around is the sea of paradise.

—THOMAS MERTON,
A YEAR WITH THOMAS MERTON

A Powerful Pause for the Days Ahead

Try to pray in this way for several days in a row. At the end of the day, review what happened and look for where God was present. Allow yourself to see and receive God beyond the ideas and things you're certain of. Ask God to show you where the divine is in your life this day.

36

No Cows to Lose

Without wonder we approach life as a self-help project.
We employ techniques; we analyze gifts and potentiali-
ties; we set goals and assess progress. Spiritual formation
is reduced to cosmetics.

—Eugene H. Peterson, *Christ Plays in*
Ten Thousand Places

One day the Buddha was sitting with his monks. A distraught farmer approached. "Monks, have you seen my cows?" The Buddha said, "No we have not." The farmer continued, "I am distraught. I have only twelve cows, and now they are gone. How will I survive?" The Buddha looked at him with compassion and said, "I'm sorry my friend, we have not seen them. You may want to look in the other direction." After the farmer had gone, the Buddha turned to his monks, looked at them deeply, smiled, and said, "Dear ones, do you know how lucky you are? You don't have any cows to lose."

This is an easy story because I don't own any cows—a few cats maybe, and one rambunctious dog. It's just that the things that do clutter my heart and mind (and absorb my energy and focus, and weigh me down) are much more encumbering than the farmer's cows.

My need to be in a hurry.

My need to impress those around me.

My dissatisfaction with ordinary days and gifts of grace.

My preoccupation with all that's left undone.

When my identity is defined by what I have, or possess, or earn, or strive for, or require in order to impress, I have *everything* to lose.

The Sabbath—stopping, sitting still, waiting—allows us to hear the voice of Grace saying, "You are accepted, period. Deal with it."

It is a reminder that I can live and choose and commit *from acceptance* and not *for acceptance*. I'm not doing any of this (Sabbath, prayer, pause, rest, reflection, renewal) to impress anyone or earn points. Life is full. *This* life, or moment, or relationship, or conversation, or encounter. The sacred present begins here.

A young man boarded an overnight train in Europe. He was told, "There has been a lot of theft recently. We take no responsibility for any loss." This worried the young man, because he had a lot of stuff. So, he lay awake, fearing the worst, staring at his stuff. Finally, at 3:00 a.m., he fell asleep. Waking with a start twenty minutes later, he saw that his stuff was gone. He took a deep breath. "Thank God," he said. "Now I can sleep."

Inspirations

Whoever has a desire to keep his life safe will have it taken from him; but whoever gives up his life because of me, will have it given back to him.

—JESUS, THE GOSPEL OF MATTHEW

～～～～～～～～～～～～～～～～～～～～

A Powerful Pause for the Days Ahead

Perhaps you don't have any cows to lose. But you probably have other things that have become the source of meaning or security or importance for you—the things that you clutch. Try to identify your cows.

37

Uncle George

If I have told you these details about the asteroid, and made a note of its number for you, it is on account of the grown-ups and their ways. . . . When you tell them that you have made a new friend, they never ask you any questions about essential matters. They never say to you, "What does his voice sound like? What games does he love best? Does he collect butterflies?" Instead, they demand: "How old is he? How many brothers has he? How much does he weigh? How much money does his father make?" Only from these figures do they think they have learned anything about him.

—Antoine De Saint-Exupéry,
The Little Prince

Uncle George was demanding and difficult. Looking after him was stressful and taxing, not to mention thankless.

Driving to the funeral of Uncle George, the young man lets loose with pent-up emotion.

"Thank God," he says to his wife. "I suppose I'm sorry he died, but I've got to tell you, I don't think I could have stood one more day with that annoying man. I've had enough. And I'm telling you that the only reason I gave so much time and energy to your Uncle George was because of my love for you!"

"*My* Uncle George," she says flabbergasted. "I thought he was *your* Uncle George!"

We collect Uncle Georges. It is the perfect metaphor for any anxiety, worry, fret, apprehension, or fear that is elevated to the level of urgent consternation. Uncle George consumes us. And he's not even our uncle.

Which means there is a shift; now I am worrying about stuff I can do nothing about. And I give my attention, energy, and time to nonessential matters.

And yet. For all our objections to the contrary, we collect worries like we collect all our stuff; there's always room for one more. It seems to take care of something. I know I like to use Uncle George to let you know how important or busy or indispensable I am.

But worry and fuss gum up the system, stop the flow. The word *worry* comes from an Anglo-Saxon word meaning "to strangle" or "to choke." It's as if we are literally cutting off the air supply that allows us to breathe emotionally and spiritually.

Preoccupied with Uncle George, I am, quite literally, not myself. I am of two minds. I am exhausted, busy, pulled in many directions, and numb, not really available for people I love. This is not to say that we can't have activities or service or work. But work that is fueled by a need to be needed or a need to prove our value is too consuming, leaving no time for rejuvenation or prayer or the quiet work of the Spirit.

So what do we do? As if we don't feel bad enough, some of us go for the willpower-on-steroids approach: "Just cut it out!" That lasts for a half hour or so, about the same amount of time I can give up serious dark chocolate.

Others opt for techno-cure. Our newspaper had an article promoting "hot gadgets to help you chill on vacation." Who knew? To think I can't relax unless I have the proper equipment. (Although, maybe they have a device that could help me remember all the stuff I forgot to worry about. And, oddly, much of my worry is second-generation worry: worrying about the stuff in the past, wondering about whether it received its quota of adequate worry.)

The bottom line? While tending to Uncle George, we lose focus. When this happened to Jesus' friends ("because so many people were coming and going that they did not even have a chance to eat," Gospel of Mark), Jesus didn't preach or lecture or lead a prayer.

The story says that immediately Jesus made the disciples get into the boat and go ahead of him to the other side, while he sent the crowds away. "Come with me by yourselves," Jesus told them, "to a quiet place and get some rest."

It is not about creating a life absent of stress. It's about being present, even in the hectic.

In other words, it is in the pause—the rest, the refueling, the "be-ing," the Sabbath—that we refocus on essential matters.

The pause allows us to be present, even in the busy, the noise, the demands, the lists.

Today I am stressed. A large group is coming tomorrow to tour our garden. So I'm walking around my garden with a different point of view. It's not surprising that I no longer see surprises or splendor in the unexpected, because now I am too focused on what is missing, and I see only defects, imperfections, and blemishes. The very things I have come to love about my garden I now see as deficiencies. This worry is gumming up the system. It is choking my sense of awe. I've lost sight of essential matters—such as watching the swallowtail butterflies do their waltz with the *Buddleia* shrub near my back deck, and feeling the breeze cool my skin on this sun-drenched afternoon.

We are sitting on our back deck, with a long to-do list to complete before the tour. "Okay," my wife says, "let's forget the other stuff and go listen to the music."

She refers to the summer music festival, our small-town version of a party. Tonight it's the band Maya Soleil; African fusion music from Zambia and Ghana saturates the air.

Ober Park is an expansive, grass-covered, natural amphitheater, encircled by grassy hillsides. The music mingles with the sound of euphoric children playing, chasing, rolling, wrestling, and laughing. Most of them are barefoot. Some of the boys, including Zach, are playing king of the hill. Around the park, people old and young are dancing. I see a mother dancing and twirling with her small child in her arms.

I remember that feeling, from my childhood, playing well into a Michigan summer night. We would catch fireflies, putting as many as we could into a mason jar, making our own lantern. "We don't have to go to bed now, do we?" we would plead, the warmth of well-being and contentment lingering in our tired bodies, fused with the sensation of grass stains itching on our arms and legs.

Here, the sunlight is still high in the sky—a sky permeated by joy, laughter, and ease. It's the first warm evening we've had in some time, and everyone is glad to be here. Introducing the next song, the female lead singer says, "Everybody, get up and rejoice. I know there's a child in you."

I still have work to do. But it can wait. Right now, this is more important. It is the heart of Sabbath. The music washes over me. And I don't give any thought to Uncle George.

Inspirations

For where your treasure is, there will your heart be also.

—JESUS, THE GOSPEL OF LUKE

~~~~~~~~~~~~~~~~~~~~~~

A Powerful Pause for the Days Ahead

To help you avoid taking on worries you can do nothing about, go on a news fast for at least a day. No news from radio, TV, or the Internet. Really.

38

Play

You can discover more about a person in an hour of play than in a year of conversation.

—PLATO

Today is an ordinary Sunday. I'm sitting at my patio table. There are remnants of the *New York Times*, an empty coffee mug, and a blank notepad with pen. My assignment is to write about play. I wrestle with the compulsion to want to say the right thing. But it gets caught up in the maelstrom of cultural expectations about performance, and this makes my head hurt. So I get another cup of coffee.

Out on the lawn, my eight-year-old son, Zach, is sketching a Western Tanager. The tanager spent the morning splashing in the pond. We don't see tanagers much, so when they make an appearance, everything else on the to-do list gets demoted.

My notepad is still blank. There is too much swirling in my head for me to organize my thoughts, so I take a break and wander down to one of my garden beds where a David Austin rose, the *Gertrude Jekyll,* has bowed to the weight of blooms, all canes akimbo, doing its best imitation of the scarecrow from *The Wizard of Oz*. It needs staking. I notice a convention of bees delighting in the hardy geranium nearby, entertaining themselves with a musical mantra, some kind of monastic a cappella tune, and I take a hit of the rose, a concoction of cloves and some unnameable soap from my childhood. On walking back to the house, I see Zach and his friend running through the sprinkler on the lawn.

They squeal—literally. Poster children for enthrallment.

They live by the philosophy that if the day doesn't have a fine game worth playing, it's a good time to make one up.

If pressed, I would say that play is living without an agenda. But that almost sounds like some kind of a dictum. And I swear by the philosophy that anytime we reduce life to a one-sentence dictum, it's time to detox.

For me, play is garden ambling, sometimes with a nine iron in my hand, to practice my golf swing and whack a couple of stray practice balls into the woods. At dusk, I listen to the birds do their makeshift choir (it's like a pickup game of baseball, whoever shows up in the woods on this night gets to sing). I have a friend who kayaks in the eddies and canals that connect all the lakes in central Florida, and another who sits on his boat around midnight out in the intercoastal waters in total darkness and listens to music, and another who hikes in the woods where the trees are the size of cathedrals and the earth smells of history and rain, and still another who goes fishing without really caring whether he catches any. After all, it's just the fishing that seems to matter.

There's a great story about a research project with children who had been put into a room with new toys. The study was to determine which toys the children enjoyed most. After twenty minutes or so of playing with all the new toys, the children spent the remainder of their time enthusiastically playing with all of the boxes that the toys came in.

I still laugh out loud when I picture it.

Children are wired to be fully alive. To see. Wired to derive joy from that which is simple. From play. It is a by-product of engagement. There is no need for stuff to entertain, or occupy, or preoccupy, or distract. There is no constraint to control.

A Greek philosopher named Heraclitus once said, "Man is most nearly himself when he achieves the seriousness of a child at play." And more recently, Scott Russell Sanders observed that "for the enlightened few, the world is always lit." Which is another way of saying that the requirement for enlightenment is pretty straightforward: let yourself live like a kid.

But somewhere along the way to adulthood, play gives way to our need to be preoccupied, distracted, and important. Remember the movie *Big*? Thirteen-year-old Josh wants to be big, and he magically gets his wish from a carnival-machine genie. He lives in the city and becomes a huge success working for a company making and selling toys. Slowly, he loses his little-boy ways and absorbs an adult perspective and demeanor, replete with busyness, stress, and the need for accomplishment. His friend Billy comes to his office with news about the machine, which (they both hope) will reverse the spell.

Josh: Will you please leave? I've got a deadline to meet.

Billy: Who . . . do you think you are?

Josh: *Hey*!

Billy: You're Josh Baskin, remember? You broke your arm on my roof! You hid in *my* basement when Robert Dyson was about to rip your head off!

Josh: You don't get it, do you? This is important!

Billy: I'm your best friend. What's more important than that, huh?

Centuries ago, desert father Abba Poemen said, "Do not give your heart to that which does not satisfy your heart." But, in point of fact, we do. We give up play for some measurement(s) designed to weigh our accomplishments. This is why we tend to make play and wasted time synonymous. We become oblivious to the Jewish heritage of Sabbath, reminding us there is one day a week set aside to literally waste time with God. (I read that Seneca, with cynicism in his pen, noted that the Jews waste one-seventh of their life.)

When we play, we romp and revel in the day's simple pleasures. This way of life is a tough sell in our important-people-have-no-free-time world. Our sophisticated technology guarantees to give us more time. Yet, in the end, we live out of breath and out of time.

We seem to lose the ability to play early in life, don't we?

And this is happening to people younger and younger. I read a recent statement by a nine-year-old boy who said he wanted to "be inside because that's where all the electrical outlets are."

There's no advantage to taking a moral high road here, but I do believe that indoor play is an oxymoron. Because play

leaves no circuit turned off. It means being alive in this world—
squarely in the sights, sounds, smells, and tastes of this day.

Like everything else, our culture has turned play into some
sort of an achievement, a contest, a beauty pageant. And in the
end, it kind of defeats the point. Someone noted that in this
culture

we worship our work,

play at our worship,

and work at our play.

We treat play as if it is a problem to be solved, and we counter
with a book on *Play for Dummies* replete with activity-appropriate
checklists. As if play is something to be accomplished. We add
play to our scores of other activities, feeling duly accomplished
with our ability to multitask.

I sit on the back deck and watch my son dance to The Mamas
and the Papas, barefoot in the grass. And there is something
wonderfully cathartic in the immersion of play that reorganizes
life's priority list. It creates a surge of well-being to the marrow
of our bones, and we know it and sense it but find ourselves
unable to describe it, or write about it, or teach it for that matter.
But this is all well and good, keeping it free from the panel of
judges that call the shots on whether life is worth living.

This much I know: Play clears the cobwebs of busyness and
public opinion. It helps us step out of that space in which we're
subjected to judgments and seductions. In today's newspaper
alone, I was invited to fret and marvel over a baby picture worth
more than $4 million; to be interested in an upswing in the
number of people who are getting liposuction, including their

knees (because we all know the humiliation of fat knees); to be reminded of a can't-miss stock pick; and to be motivated to buy a book that will allow me to visualize a new me in just seven days.

No. Play happens in another space entirely, where music, laughter, friendship, and wonder are birthed and nourished.

Inspirations

It will be gone before you know it. The fingerprints on the wall appear higher and higher. Then suddenly they disappear.

—DOROTHY EVSLIN

A Powerful Pause for the Days Ahead

Run through a sprinkler, or

roll down a hill, or

swing on a swing, or

play in sand, or—you know what to do.

⁓ **Play** like a child. Visit www.loyolapress.com/ powerofpause and click on Book Extras to find instructions for making pinwheels, suncatchers, tambourines, and other whimsical crafts.

39

For Ordinary Time: Ordinary Bliss

There is a slight lifting of the air so I can smell the earth
for the first time, and yesterday I again took possession
of my life here.

—MAY SARTON, *ENCORE: A JOURNAL OF*
THE EIGHTIETH YEAR

We should do this more often." A middle-aged man is speaking to a woman standing at his side. I am doing what I do best: eavesdropping.

The couple is leaning on the upper-deck railing of a Washington State ferry. We are headed across the Puget Sound, from Seattle toward the Kitsap Peninsula. The Olympic Mountains, still snow tipped, fill our panorama. I have lived in this neck of the woods almost twenty years, and this tranquil scene—a melding of pewter blue water with a hunter green tree line—has not yet failed to give me goose bumps. Whenever I return from a trip, the mountains and water always reorient me. Listening and watching this couple, it is apparent that they, too, are plumb tickled, finding enchantment and solace in nature's pageant.

"We should do what?" she asks.

"Take these mini vacations," he tells her as he gestures. "Take time to enjoy all of this. We need to slow down, get out and about."

"But we're doing it right now," the woman offers.

"Yes," the husband persists, "but think of all the opportunities and years we've missed."

And I think (but do not say), *Keep talking, and you'll miss this one.*

We all practice a finely honed skill: expecting life to reside in an event or experience other than the one we are in right now.

There are those lucky moments when we recognize and embrace the here and now. But I'll be if we don't want to bottle it up and sell it on eBay. (This makes me think of the Transfiguration story in the Gospel of Mark—Peter's so worked up with goose bumps he wants to build three condos and call it permanent). Or worse yet, we feel compelled to evaluate or measure each experience, as if a superlative is required for its enjoyment.

Brian called me this morning with "an exciting opportunity." His name didn't ring a bell, but Brian chatted as if he knew me well. And, it's not every day you get offered an exciting opportunity. Brian wanted me to have a free satellite dish. All for me. This kind of generosity makes you all tingly inside, doesn't it? I could get five hundred channels, Brian told me. And all these options provide me "so much more to enjoy in life," Brian chirped (literally, he chirped). And (Brian's spiel had no pause button) I would never have to be "afraid of missing anything," because I could TiVo all the good stuff. I didn't want to burden Brian with the fact that being faced with a lot of options—like standing in the grocery store trying to choose cereal or toothpaste—makes me want to beat my head against a metal pole, so five hundred channels might send me straight to the floor in a fetal position. Instead, I told Brian that while I was "in awe" of his offer, I would like to make my decision after I spent some time deadheading my roses, filling my bird feeders, and taking a brief nap in my lawn chair. Brian was quiet. I'm not sure he understood.

While waiting for perfect, we pass on ordinary.

While waiting for better, we don't give our best effort to good.

While waiting for new and improved, we leach the joy right out of the old and reliable.

There's nothing wrong with looking forward to something. Like my friend who likes to say, "I'm not going to have a midlife crisis until I can afford to buy a Mustang." Fair enough.

But most of the time, Alfred E. Neuman is right, "Most of us don't know what we want in life, but we're sure that we haven't got it."

In a culture of lottery winners and bigger and louder and faster and newer and shinier, ordinary gets lost in the din. Ordinary, like watching dusk settle while reading in my favorite chair, counting nuthatches when they return to the feeder, enjoying a handful of fresh strawberries (they sit on the tongue with a sweetness that makes you believe in heaven), and wrestling with my son on the back lawn. Ordinary, yes. But a day without the heaviness of expectation, worry, or fear.

I read this in a wonderful book called *Children's Letters to God*. Sara writes: "Dear God, I didn't think orange went with purple, until I saw the sunset You made on Tuesday. That was cool."

That's the spirit, Sara.

A Powerful Pause for the Days Ahead

Find a coloring book and some crayons or colored pencils. Allow yourself the ordinary bliss of adding color to a page. Allow your childhood self to be here and enjoy it. If you are brave, color this page in the book.

PART SEVEN

Early Autumn

40

Shadows

As long as the most important thing in your life is to keep finding your way, you're going to live in mortal terror of losing it. Once you're willing to be lost, though, you'll be home free.

—ROBERT CAPON, *KINGDOM, GRACE, JUDGMENT*

I've missed all my deadlines for the past seven weeks, including this project.

I shrugged it off and added it to a growing catalog of discontent: stalled projects, lack of motivation, unmet commitments, a nagging unease ("this day is not what I signed on for"), a desire to sleep past noon, and a mood the shade of indigo. "Okay," my friend reminds me, "so life is hard. You want to talk with the complaint department, take a number."

Have you ever felt unmoored? I have. And I do. Things had been going well, but something derailed. I hit a wall. I tell myself, "There's got to be a pill for this." What is the use of receiving two hundred spam e-mails a day, if not to take advantage of every offer of chemicals and other things that will make life a stroll in the park?

Melancholy is only made worse by our cultural expectations to rise above it. "Don't let on," people will say. Or if you do, tell the story as if this is a problem already resolved: "I used to struggle with that, but not anymore." The other day, when flying to some destination, I reflected on all of this. I noticed that the woman next to me was reading a magazine article guaranteed to "Tone Thighs, Butt and Abs." Maybe that's the secret—a toned butt. I caught myself reading over her shoulder.

Sedona, Arizona, is famous for red rock. On this particular morning, the air is cool and the sky saturated with light. Its blue shade thins, as if God painted the morning using watercolor. I sit on my hotel balcony, coffee in hand, and gaze at the rock faces. Only when I look carefully do I notice the shadows. Without any trees or shrubs growing on them, these red rocks appear as an ancient face that is etched with wisdom creases, like a Navajo chief. Each crease holds a shadow, and each demarcation proves malleable, shifting as sunlight washes over the mountain.

Each crease has its story, too. From where I sit, it looks like scarred wood that's been etched by time and wind and rain and shifting earth—in some cases a violent confluence of water and fate and history. Born of a convulsive past, these rock outcroppings have no choice but to be bold, arresting, and unabashed. But their beauty, their nuance, is in the shadows.

It is the shadows that give credence, gravitas, substance, and appeal. Over and against these pockets of shade, the face of red rock stands out. In relief, exposed to the unforgiving heat of the sun, it is the color of rust.

To make sense of the geology is beyond my pay grade and intellectual capacity. It is enough to know that, according to intelligent people, it all started about 320 million years ago (give or take a few million) with a drama befitting a Greek stage—expanses lying first under water, then eroded and thus created by ancient rivers, which deposited the sandstone, resulting in today's red palette. (It was all the same upheaval that created the Grand Canyon.) Today, in Sedona, we have Bell Rock, Courthouse Butte, Cathedral Rock, Coffee Pot Rock, and Steamboat Rock, all unique and inimitable cliff faces, etched by the vicissitudes of history.

What I can clearly see is that this place comes alive, exquisitely and excessively alive, because of these pockets of shade. These dark containers are like the pauses between the notes in a Mozart adagio. In these spaces, there is silence . . . and beauty born of anguish.

In these rocks, the shadow lines are beautiful. But I am less optimistic about the shadows in my own life. Shadows are those parts that we hide, either consciously or unconsciously. They can be disappointment, doubt, sorrow, disillusion, insecurity, disenchantment, nonfulfillment, heartache, or shame. Why do we feel constrained to eradicate these lines? Why buy creams guaranteed to make us look like Nicole Kidman and workout equipment to make us feel like the Terminator?

The combination of these exaggerated cultural hopes and my own skewed expectations produces a dangerous hunger: I want to be rescued from my shadows—by some event or person or experience. So I find myself starting sentences with, "I wish that . . ." or "If only . . ."

I have bought into the notion that my well-being and my contentment are contingent upon my getting past this place. I feel compelled to escape this time, this yearning, this sorrow, this sense of unease. I reject my shadows.

I do this by telling myself that whatever I am experiencing is certainly temporary, and therefore, not my "real world." There is a cultural sleight of hand (the trick of all good magicians and cultural keepers of public decorum) that tricks us into focusing on the wrong object. We want to avoid the discomfort and go directly to the solution.

If I see the shadow as an indictment that brings shame, or a blemish to be eradicated, or a piece of bad luck to be prayed away, I devote all my mental energy and expendable income on cosmetic improvement. How do I look?

I was weaned on the notion that praying was sort of like putting coins in a slot machine. It goes well with the American notion that God exists solely for my well-being and mood disorders. What else is God going to do with her time, if not make Americans happy?

My friend, talking about her own shadows, said, "This never goes away. It never gets any easier. How do people cope?" I understand. We want to return to some place of invincibility or invulnerability. We want to return to a place where hope still has power, where we can still feel that all of life is ahead of us.

So, too easily and too quickly we dismiss our creases and shadows—places of reluctance, uncertainty, ambiguity, confusion, angst, grief, loss, fear, shame, or passion. We see them only as darkness. And hope becomes a sort of lottery ticket, something that might just click this time and make everything change.

But what if hope is really about the Incarnation—God (literally) with us? In the midst? In the middle of? In—as in, this life and these shadows? What if this shadow—the long night with no destination in sight, and with only a stone for a pillow—is where we encounter the truth? "Surely the Lord is in this place and I did not know it" (Genesis 28:16).

I learn from people who do not divorce their faith journey from their times of "unmooring." Henri Nouwen, for instance. Toward the end of his life, he moved to Toronto to live in the L'Arche Daybreak community, a community of homes for mentally challenged adults and their caregivers. At L'Arche, Nouwen was among people who wanted his love, not his lectures. Working with these adults, Nouwen was no longer able to rely on his intellectual expertise. Two years later, at age fifty-five, he experienced a six-month crisis. He wrote: "Everything came crashing down—my self-esteem, my energy to live and work, my sense of being loved, my hope for healing, my trust in God . . . everything" (*The Inner Voice of Love*).

From this place of shadows, a renewed sense of self emerged for Nouwen, one that was more authentic, more himself. He learned the difference between "being productive and being fruitful" through the downward mobility of living in community and not the upward mobility of academia.

Our enemy is clear: the notion that another life, a different life from the one I am living now, will take care of any problem. In her memoir *A Three Dog Life*, Abigail Thomas wrote: *"If only life were more like this,* you will think, as you and the dogs traipse up to bed, and then you realize with a start that this *is* life."

Back on my Sedona patio, the sun has almost disappeared behind the red rocks. In the dusk there are no shadows, and the outcropping faces appear flatter, less dimensional. My wish is granted: there are no more shadows. But the cost is too much. It is clear to me that, in these places of unspeakable grandeur, it is the scars, the wounds, these great slashes from time, and the elements of nature that draw me. They invite and hold me, create a safe place and comfort me.

If I am willing, the shadows will teach me something.

~~~~~~~~~~~~~~~~~~~~~~~~

A Powerful Pause for the Days Ahead

On a bright day (or maybe a moonlit night), go outdoors and sit in the shade of a tree. As the tree's shadow rests on you, think of your own shadows—or maybe just one of them. Just meditate on what that shadow might mean to your life. Don't try to come up with any answers. Allow the peace of the tree's shade to bring peace to your heart, shadows and all.

41

Without a List

This is my real world, where life proceeds at its own healthy pace, where I can revel in the luxury of paying more attention to sunrise and sunset than to clock time.

—KATHLEEN NORRIS, *DAKOTA: A SPIRITUAL GEOGRAPHY*

Just then there was strong wind.

It blew the list out of Toad's hand. The list blew high into the air.

"Help!" cried Toad. "My list is blowing away. What will I do without my list?"

"Hurry!" said Frog. "We will run and catch it."

"No!" shouted Toad, "I cannot do that."

"Why not?" asked Frog.

"Because," wailed Toad, "running after my list is not one of the things that I wrote on my list of things to do!"

—ARNOLD LOBEL, *FROG AND TOAD TOGETHER*

On a flight home late last night, my mind raced with the impending checklist. (I had been gone long enough to be "behind.") So I woke this autumn morning, steeling myself, ready to tackle whatever waited in the heap on my desk. The deluge of email—requests, demands, expectations—exacerbates my dilemma and raises the bar for my morning. Now, suddenly, everything is *urgent*. And my blood pressure doubles.

Why are checklists important to people? What do they take care of in me?

This morning I step outside and stand on my patio. The air in my garden has an autumn fragrance, which carries a willing acquiescence. It is a visceral sense of slowing down, the garden readying itself, gladly, for dormancy. I take a deep breath. My compulsion (or appetite) for urgency leaves me. And I am glad to be alive.

I drink my coffee sitting on a boulder at the edge of the pond. The lawn and garden are littered with debris from last night's windstorm. I pick up some of the bigger branches and throw them on the compost heap. I fill the bird feeders, noting a couple of nuthatches on nearby fir trees waiting and a bit bothered. And I remember the Benedictine teaching, that work and play and prayer are all pieces of the same life.

My summer garden carries with it a persistent list. (Time is short, so complete this. Do that. Accomplish this. Take care of that.) But the list loses it urgency in autumn. This is a time to savor. The clumps of *Pennisetum* grass near the pond are now the color of mustard. Seed heads of the taller *Miscanthus* bow, literally deferential, as if in a posture of prayer. The maple leaves have turned a soft scarlet. My worries float up into the autumn air.

A reporter interviewing a 104-year-old woman asked, "And what do you think is the best thing about being 104?"

She replied, "No peer pressure."

And it reminded me that worry and urgency are the peer pressures of my world. Urgency is predicated on our need to overcome, tidy up, fix, or cope. It has something to do with control, I suppose. And I wonder what kind of control I need, and what does it feed? And what am I so afraid of?

Not long ago I was at the Gardens and Grace Conference in Baltimore, where the Cathedral of the Incarnation has a lovely outdoor blue-slate courtyard, surrounded by shrubs and trees. The patio was littered with yellow leaves dropped from the nearby trees. The scattered, random leaves were exquisite, giving the impression of something playful and whimsical. I heard a noise, all too familiar, as a custodian carried out his assignment to blow the leaves off the patio. After ten minutes, the patio was "clean" and ready for use.

When he finished, and there was no one else around, I picked up a few handfuls of leaves and scattered them onto the patio. Letting go of urgency (for the purpose of rest and renewal) is intentional.

Inspirations

John Killinger once asked Sister Corita Kent, a nun known as a leader of worship, to help lead worship services. He received a postcard a few days later that simply said, "Dear, I am trying to be quiet. S. Corita."

A Powerful Pause for the Days Ahead

I'm giving you permission to give up urgency, if even for a day. If you have a patio, scatter some leaves. If there's a pond nearby, sit on a rock and sip your coffee. This is not an assignment. It is all about healing that place where urgency so often develops. If none of this helps, you can always make a list. Item one on the list: today, I want to lose the list.

42

The Seven Wonders of the World

Sell your cleverness and buy bewilderment.

—RUMI

The first-grade class was given an assignment: to name the seven wonders of the world. Each student compiled a list and shared it with the class. There was ardent interaction as the students called out entries from their lists: the Pyramids, the Empire State Building, the Amazon River, Yellowstone National Park, the Grand Canyon, the Taj Mahal, and so on. The teacher served as cheerleader. "Class, these are great answers. Well done!"

But one girl sat silent. The teacher asked about her list, and the girl answered, "I don't think I understand the assignment."

"Why?"

"I don't have any of the right answers."

"Well, why don't you tell us what you wrote on your paper, and we'll help you."

"Okay," said the little girl, "I think the seven wonders of the world are . . . to see, to hear, to touch, to smell, to feel, to love, to belong."

Somewhere along the way, we have buried this little girl's wisdom.

Today, I heard a radio ad for some technological toy. I call it a toy—they call it a necessity. The ad told me that I needed it. That in fact my life is not fulfilled because I don't yet own this product. The ad told me that important and productive and superior and prestigious (and very good-looking) people use this product.

The ad asked me how I'd lived this long without their product, saying essentially, "How can you possibly live?"

Then I heard another ad. It told me that God wants me rich. Really rich. Not only that, he wants me to get rich in a hurry. Of course, I had to buy someone's product first. Evidently, God wants him rich first.

Okay. They've made their point. Apparently, without their stuff I am unimportant, and my life is confined to the mundane.

But then I'm in luck. I heard another ad that promises to eliminate the mundane. What are the odds? Apparently, according to the ad, the mundane is something to be feared, and we can easily eliminate it. I was doing a conference where people were sharing their opinions about life. One woman stood and said, "Life is so . . . (she was struggling to find the right word) life is so . . . daily."

There's the problem. Life is so *daily*. No wonder we're easily tempted by one ad after another. We're trying to escape ordinary, daily life. In our rush to avoid the mundane, we miss the miracles of the ordinary.

How do we find the miracles in ordinary life? The spiritual life begins with this simple sentence: "I never noticed that before." We have to remember how to wonder, or as the little girl said, how to see, to hear, to touch, to smell, to feel, to love, to belong. When we do that, we learn to delight in the wonders of the world that are right here, right now.

Inspirations

Days pass and the years vanish and we walk sightless among miracles. Lord, fill our eyes with seeing and our minds with knowing. Let there be moments when your Presence, like lightning, illumines the darkness in which we walk. Help us to see, wherever we gaze, that the bush burns, unconsumed. And we, clay touched by God, will reach out for holiness and exclaim in wonder, "How filled with awe is this place and we did not know it."

—*MISHKAN TEFILAH*, JEWISH SABBATH PRAYER BOOK

A Powerful Pause for the Days Ahead

Try this. Sometime today, stop what you're doing. And listen. I believe you can hear the voice of that little girl reminding you of the seven wonders of the world.

43

Fully Alive

It costs so much to be a full human being that there are very few who have the enlightenment, or the courage, to pay the price. One has to abandon altogether the search for security, and reach out to the risk of living with both arms. One has to embrace the world like a lover, and yet demand no easy return of love. One has to accept pain as a condition of existence. One has to court doubt and darkness as the cost of knowing. One needs a will stubborn in conflict, but apt always to the total acceptance of every consequence of living and dying.

—MORRIS WEST,
THE SHOES OF THE FISHERMAN

In Maggie Jackson's book *Distracted: The Erosion of Attention and the Coming Dark Age*, Sherry Turkle recounts a visit she made with her teenage daughter to a Darwin exhibit at the American Museum of Natural History.

At the entrance of the show stood a cage with two grand Galapagos tortoises. Feeling sorry for the tortoises and completely unmoved by the wonder of their presence, Turkle's daughter remarked that the museum could just as well have used robots. Other children in line agreed, to their parent's dismay.

Intrigued, Turkle returned again and again to interview visitors to the exhibit and found that for most children "aliveness doesn't seem worth the trouble," and seems to have no intrinsic value. Moreover, if a realistic robotic tortoise was used instead, the children didn't think people needed to be told.

I shake my head in bemusement. But I get it. Using a robot is easier, and not just for Galapagos tortoises. I have done the same thing with my own emotional and spiritual life.

It works. It's a good way to protect myself.

This story about the tortoises resonates because I have had some conversations this week with friends about fear—the fear that comes from being real. To love at all (anything in life) is to be vulnerable.

What troubles me is how easy it is to feel afraid. Afraid of the very things—thoughts, feelings, desires, passions, yearnings, creative impulses, callings—that God put inside of me.

So I protect myself. I become robotic. I may feel, yearn, or desire, but am afraid because I don't believe there is a safe place for me—or for that part of me. I see these desires as an indictment of me for being weak, and therefore no place in which God can live.

It reminds me of the dean's speech, at the school where Patch Adams studied medicine: "Our job is to rigorously and ruthlessly train the humanity out of you and make you into something better. We're gonna make doctors out of you."

I heard Brian McLaren talk about the Genesis creation story. It says that God created and called it good. Notice this: God did not call it perfect. Meaning what? Meaning that if it were perfect, we would merely be a maintenance crew. Instead, we are very active cocreators in the process of the ongoing and unfolding of God's presence in the world.

This means that we approach life with open arms, vulnerable. Or, in the words of Alan Jones, author of *Reimagining Christianity*, "I want to know if joy, curiosity, struggle, and compassion bubble up in a person's life. I'm interested in being fully alive."

That's what I am trying for tonight, sitting in my living room, looking out the glass doors. There is a fire in the fireplace. Our "Bloodgood" Japanese maple has dropped (or conceded, some sort of autumn offering) a third of its leaves. Our patio is darker from the sheen of rain, which continues to fall softly. The stone is now a deeper, almost melancholy blue, and the fallen leaves form a tousled mound, like an embankment. It looks from where I sit as if the leaves are an intentional frame, to demarcate the deep blood red from the steel blue of the stone. It is dusk, colors that call for reflection, stopping, sitting, and absorbing. I feel, fully, the sense of autumn resignation, but take immense joy in the fusion of color, blood red, blue green leaves of *Euphorbia*, and the deep hunter green of an upright yew shrub.

I'm not sure if my fears have abated. But I know this: they are not nearly as important as they were earlier today.

A Powerful Pause for the Days Ahead

Take a risk with someone: tell them how special they are.

44

Inner Rebel

*This tension stimulated the gland of entertainment in
me and I found myself in the role of master of revels, the
evening fool, with cards in my sleeves and a ready joke
for every interval of silence. I hated myself in this role,
yet I was incapable of refusing the performance.*

—PAT CONROY, THE PRINCE OF TIDES

While I was watching an infomercial the other night (I know, you must be wondering whether I actually have a life), one testimonial made me sit up and take notice. Said one besotted consumer, "This has let me be the person I always wanted to be. Because I deserved a better life."

What is this? It's a program to earn thousands of dollars a month on some secret real-estate formula. I thought about calling the 800 number. Why? Because I, too, deserve a better life! But pouting and kvetching doesn't become me, so I decided to write about the inner rebel.

The undeniable truth? There are times when we are no longer who we thought we were going to be. Not to worry, there are endless sources—ads, commentators, preachers, TV shows—to reinforce our discontent, each of them trying to tell us who we are. They're not very subtle.

And here's the message they all have in common: Who I am now is not enough. This life isn't enough. I need another life—preferably a radically different one from the life I'm actually living.

There's always something else we need, or should buy. It subconsciously becomes a part of almost every conversation. Like last week, on the phone with a representative from the company handling my (dial-up) internet connection.

Can you get cable? she asked.

No, I answer.

Can you get DSL? she asked.

No, I answer.

Do you have a satellite dish? she asked.

No, I answer.

Silence. Wow, she said with empathy. I feel sorry for you.

I was watching a major league baseball playoff game on television (Go Detroit Tigers!), when here came an ad for a new Native American casino near Seattle. The ad invited me to visit, because there, at the casino, I am told, I will "Rediscover the Real Washington." Oh. Now that is news. The real world is in a casino! In the meantime, in my "unreal" Washington, outside my study window, a full moon hangs in the southern sky, and the chill in the autumn air heralds a changing season—the night air now smelling of leaves and the burning wood from fireplaces.

It is all fuel for the race. We are hurried, multitasking, market-conscious consumers. And the race always wins.

> When (we) were born, (we) were allowed to enjoy the solid, nutritious food of life—namely, work, play, fun, laughter, the company of people, the pleasure of the senses and the mind. (We) were given a taste for the drug called approval, appreciation, attention. . . . Having a taste for these drugs, we became addicted and began to dread losing them. (Henri Nouwen, in online lecture on leadership)

By my count, there are too many folk claiming to know God who fuel the fire. I watched a TV preacher talk about God's will as if our lives are paint by number. He asked, "Are you sure (emphasis on *sure*) you are in God's will today?" This kind of stuff encourages a fear-fueled introspection that leads to an even more hurried lifestyle doing whatever we can to buy God's forgiveness.

To go against the flow of such messages requires that we become, literally, rebels. Like writer Ellen Meloy's brother, who was expelled from Sunday school for coloring Jesus' face purple. Apparently, Jesus' face can't be purple. Who knew?

There's a simple test. If the voices (from culture, Madison Avenue, religious gurus, self-help teachers, or concerned onlookers) leach the awe, wonder, joyfulness, playfulness, and generosity from your life, it is pure snake oil. Have no part of it. The end result is disheartenment, discouragement, a loss of focus, and a frenzied lifestyle accumulating whatever it is we're supposed to need to get back in the good graces of God or of public opinion.

We could benefit from the wisdom and council of Thomas Merton, who argued,

> There is a pervasive form of contemporary violence (and that is) activism and overwork. . . . The rush and pressure of modern life are a form of violence . . . To allow oneself to be carried away by a multitude of conflicting concerns, to surrender to too many demands, to commit oneself to too many projects, to want to help everyone in everything, is to succumb to violence. The frenzy of our activism neutralizes our work for peace. It destroys our inner capacity for peace. It destroys the fruitfulness of our won work, because it kills the root of inner wisdom which makes work fruitful. (*Conjectures of a Guilty Bystander*)

So where do we go? What is the alternative? Where do we find this fuel for a sense of self? I need to ask myself the same question I ask anyone who seeks my opinion about any of life's conundrums: Where do you hear the voice of Grace? Seriously.

And when did you hear it last?

And are you willing to be loved for being *this* you, not some fantasy you created in the boardroom of an ad agency?

> I was a neurotic for years. I was anxious and depressed and selfish. Everyone kept telling me to change. I resented them, and I agreed with them, and I wanted to change, but

simply couldn't, no matter how hard I tried. . . . Then one day, he said to me, "Don't change. I love you just as you are." Those words were music to my ears: "Don't change. Don't change. Don't change . . . I love you as you are." I relaxed. I came alive. And suddenly I changed! (Anthony de Mello, *In the Song of the Bird*)

Recently I watched the 1991 Harrison Ford movie, *Regarding Henry*, about a genuine SOB lawyer who is shot in a random accident. After that, he's not the same mentally, physically, or spiritually. During his rehabilitation, he has a friendship with Bradley, his physical therapist. The lawyer says, "I thought I could go back to my life, but I don't like who I was, Bradley. . . . I don't fit in."

Bradley says, "I got bad knees. Football, wrecked 'em both playing college football. Man, that was my life. What else was there. . . . safety hit me . . . game over, my life was over . . . ask me if I mind having bad knees. No way. I had to find a life. Don't listen to nobody trying to tell you who you are."

There will always be someone who wants us to choose a label for our identity—you know, "I'm codependent or dysfunctional or an addict or high-powered or successful or . . ."— and every single one of them is limiting. Why not simply, "I am the light of the world"? When Jesus said, "you are the light of the world," he did not say (borrowing from Wayne Muller), "let your light shine only if you grew up in a loving, supportive, two-parent biological family and had no sorrow in your life . . . or if you were never violated or harmed, or if you never had illness or grief."

Today, I am walking the paths in my autumn garden. The garden carries a sense of resignation. As if it, like the rest of us, is giving in to the inevitable, cooler weather on the way. My roses, yet with blooms, bow, deferential, weighted with dew. In the house I hear music. My son, Zach, is playing The Band and dancing. I laugh out loud.

Awareness plus gratitude places you squarely in this world, and in the life you have. It's called the sacrament of the present moment. And for this moment, it is enough.

***

A Powerful Pause for the Days Ahead

Find a place where people are in a hurry, rushing around. Sit and watch—not to judge but to notice what happens when hurry consumes us. Is there anyone who is not in a hurry? When you're consumed by this sense of hurry, how does it play out on the inside? What does it make you feel?

45

Love or Fear?

God is spreading grace around in the world like a five-year-old spreads peanut butter, thickly, sloppily, eagerly, and if we are in the back shed trying to stay clean, we won't even get a taste.

—DONNA SCHAPER, QUOTED IN
*A HUNDRED WAYS TO KEEP
YOUR SOUL ALIVE*

The air is crisp; it's one of those autumn mornings when the air itself is best mainlined, like a shot of adrenalin. Any languor from the summer heat (if you call what we have in Seattle heat) has migrated south. I am at the Village Green at our Saturday market. A sizeable crowd is milling, talking, lolling, selling, buying; everyone seems energized, enthused, glad to be here, on this day, this morning. Many, like me, have nowhere to be and nothing in particular to do. If we had a to-do list, we left it at home. Or the dog ate it.

There's a band playing, a gathering of local musicians: drums, guitar, synthesizer, and saxophone. They're playing

"Secret Agent Man." I'm not making this up—here in this place we are happily frozen in another decade. If you squint and look out at the crowd, you will see it all in tie-dye.

I'm sitting on a picnic-table bench, and my mind is doing its typical meander.

I remember a newspaper article I read earlier this morning, a report following the devastation of Hurricane Katrina and the exaggerated fears that multiplied. The chief of police had stated publically: "Tourists are being robbed and raped. In the Superdome, gangs are killing and raping women and children." It turns out that these statements were not true. They were mere perceptions that, in the end, became toxic and fueled by fear. The article went on to say that the fear provoked a change in behavior. "The fear changed strike deployment; it delayed medical evacuations; it drove police officers to quit; and it grounded helicopters."

That's what fear does. It rearranges our world.

Fear is not an unfamiliar emotion to a boy raised in a fundamentalist church. I've knelt at many altar rails, committing myself to missionary service or rededicating myself to a life without lust (which meant, for a teenager, frequent trips to the rail). There is nothing wrong with either commitment, but in my case, they were not in response to a gracious invitation, but always in mortal fear of what the almighty God would do to me.

I believe there are times when we treat God no differently from how we would relate to an alcoholic father. We walk on eggshells, eager for a smile but expecting the ax to fall. Here is the difference between living from love and living from fear. If I live in fear (or by fear or from fear), then I short-circuit my ability to invest in or commit to life—to *this* life. I become protective and insular. Fear sets the agenda and determines my course.

In fear . . .

I do not act; I react.

I do not risk; I hedge my bets.

I do not love; I clutch.

I do not take responsibility; I blame others.

And, to make matters worse, in fear, we create enemies where there are none. There's a great story from sometime around the Civil War. A physician in the South argued that slaves were suffering from two forms of mental illness. He named them Drapetomania and dysaethesia aethiopica. What are the symptoms of these mental illnesses?

Are you ready for this? Apparently these slaves suffered from an uncontrollable urge to escape, disobey their masters, and refuse to work.

So that's it. If it rattles our preconceptions, we fear it, label it, and dismiss it. We don't understand it, we fear it. If we fear it, we call it a sickness.

I read once that love is what we're born with, and fear is what we learn here.

So, how do we live without fear?

A woman did just that, in a story from the Gospel of Luke. She crashed a party. She was not invited. And you could tell by what she was wearing that she did not do "church work"—the black lace gave her away. She carried a jar of perfume. She knelt before Jesus and washed his feet with the perfume, then dried his feet with her hair. For a woman to let down her hair in first-century Israel was an extravagant, risk-taking gesture. It was considered immoral. A religious leader at the table with Jesus caught the significance. "Jesus, if you were really a prophet, you'd know who this woman is. She's a prostitute, single, from a dysfunctional family, and probably is really a Samaritan!"

That's what fear does. It labels. It dismisses.

But Jesus replied, "You don't understand. A prophet sees more than the way things are. He sees the way they become. And this woman will be remembered through all of history for her act of kindness."

Jesus reinforced her identity based on love.

Love can cost a lot, but not loving always costs more, and those who fear to love often find that want of love is an emptiness that robs life of its joy.

The band is still playing, a song I recognize but cannot name. Two small children dance (well, bounce or hop or jump with the beat), unrestrained. A grandfather mirrors his young granddaughter's steps, their delight resplendent. Contagious. These children still see relationships built on trust, not fear. And I see it clearly: she dances because she is not afraid.

She dances because she is not afraid.

Inspirations

Do not be afraid.

—JESUS, THE GOSPEL OF MATTHEW

A Powerful Pause for the Days Ahead

I think that fear is all about what we feed. Take a little time this week to ponder these questions:

Which worries or fears are taking up more time in my life than they are worth?

Which worries or fears do I encourage by giving them so much of my attention?

PART EIGHT

Late Autumn

46

Glory in the Gray

*The great lesson from the true mystics . . . is that the
sacred is in the ordinary, that it is to be found in one's
daily life, in one's neighbors, friends, and family, in
one's back yard.*

—ABRAHAM MASLOW, *THE FARTHER
REACHES OF HUMAN NATURE*

In the Pacific Northwest, where I live, gray is not a metaphor.
Gray is real. Gray is our canopy, our sky, the garment of our
psyche.

Like Eskimos with snow, we find that one word does not
do it justice. So we have gun-metal gray. Confederate gray. Ash
gray. Thundercloud gray. High-school locker gray. Lead gray.
And, for those special days, sullen gray. After time, gray becomes
the lens, the filter, through which we see, interpret, and translate
our reality.

To call us pessimists is overly simplistic. Besides, there's
something to be said for pessimists. I believe that an optimist
is merely someone who does not have all the information.

Pessimists, on the other hand, are realists who have merely forgotten to take their medication.

Or, we could use a lesson from Pooh. Winnie-the-Pooh is riding his honey pot down the river. "I ought to say that it isn't just an ordinary sort of boat," Pooh says. "Sometimes it's a Boat, and sometime it's more of an Accident. It all depends."

"Depends on what?" asks Piglet.

"On whether I'm on top of it or underneath it," says Pooh (*Winnie-the-Pooh*, by A. A. Milne).

In the midst of writing this piece, I needed to call customer service at a computer-related company, to ask questions about an inadvertent charge on my bill. After ten full minutes of "if you want this, press 1," "if you want that, press 2," "if you want to talk with a real person, press fat chance," I debated giving my computer to Goodwill.

Finally, I reach a person in customer service. Her voice is accented. After two sentences it is obvious: either she's not understanding me, or I'm not understanding her.

"Where are you?" I ask.

"India," she tells me.

"The country?" I ask.

"Yes."

It takes a minute for this to register.

"Do you have the name of someone I could talk with here? Someone local, who knows the situation about islands and the area where I live?" I ask.

"Yes," she says.

"Can I have that name and number?" I ask, feeling hopeful.

"No," she says. "We're not at liberty to say."

"So you do have names and numbers of people in customer service here on the west coast of the United States?" I ask to clarify.

"Yes, but we're not at liberty to give you their names."

"How do I reach them?" I ask.

"I don't know, sir," she says. "Is there anything else I can help you with?"

I hang up, doing my best to hold in my frustration and ire but feeling that I've sprung a leak somewhere. I leave my office and sit a spell in the garden. The sun is warm and restorative. There is something about fresh air, sun, and the way the shafts of light hit the limbs of the cedar tree that brings perspective.

And I remember a sentence from Esther de Waal. "It is such a very simple thing to walk through life with my hands open, my eyes open, listening, alive in all my five senses to God breaking in again and again on my daily life."

Okay. But how do we reconcile these two perspectives?

My world is, all too often, gray. And yet, God is in the gray. It doesn't quite compute.

In addition, we all know that gray isn't just weather related. We live in a world out of breath and out of time. We live in a world that preaches a gospel of exhaustion. Over a century ago, John Ruskin wrote: "Every increased possession loads us with a new weariness."

Imagine what he would say now. Now that we have specific stores dedicated solely to products indispensable for the purpose of storing other products. We buy stuff in order to store more stuff. (Yes, this sounds like enlightenment to me.)

Many people are all too eager to tell me how to solve this "gray dilemma." "You need to look on the bright side," they tell me. Nothing gets my goat like someone who assumes that their mission in life is to cheer me up. "Don't worry, you'll feel better soon," they tell me. "Don't worry, be happy."

I don't deny that this type of therapy works, but only if and when it is Bob Marley singing it, and the CD is blaring while I lounge on a beach somewhere near the equator, holding a beverage possessing one of those goofy umbrellas.

And this I know from experience: nothing is worse than manufactured good cheer.

This is not a call to rework or reimagine reality. Standing at my study window, incanting, "This is not rain, this is not rain, this is not rain . . ." No. Not only is this rain, this is Noah redux, and we're googling "ark building plans." We have begun to pick two of each animal . . .

We find meaning only when we enter this life, this moment—this gray. God is to be found not by stepping aside from the flow of daily life (by trying to recreate religious moments and environments, or by looking away from creation to a spiritual realm beyond), but rather by entering attentively the depths of the present moment.

And there, we find the truth of Hildegard of Bingen: "Every creature is a glittering, glistening mirror of divinity."

Last Sunday afternoon I wandered my garden. It was already deluged; we've had record rainfall. But the air on this morning was clear, the sky visible after a morning shower. Off to the west, there were breaks in the clouds, and layers of blue. I stifled my compulsion to prune or trim. I smiled at the beauty of the skeletal framework of all the deciduous plants, now naked. The dogwoods still possessed a few stubborn leaves, like Post-it notes suspended in the breeze. I absorbed the comfort of this walk. There was something in the embrace, the slowed pace.

And then yesterday it snowed, several inches, which is a big deal in this neck of the woods. It shut down our island for the most part. Our roads are now skating rinks. Zach seems oblivious. He bundles up and shouts, "Who's going to come out and play with me?" Outside my window I see him running as best he can through the backyard, his face lifted, eyes closed, tongue extended as far as is possible. What is he doing in this gray? He is catching snowflakes.

Inspirations

Follow truth wherever you find it. Even if it takes you outside your preconceived ideas of God or life. Even if it takes you outside your own country into most insignificant alien places like Bethlehem.

—GEORGE MACLEOD,
DAILY READINGS WITH GEORGE MACLEOD

A Powerful Pause for the Days Ahead

Where is the gray in your life? Why do we avoid the gray? In what ways could you enter it this week?

47

Making Space to Hear the Heart

Hobbes (leaning against a tree with Calvin): When you're confronted with the stillness of nature you can even hear yourself think.
Calvin: This is making me nervous. Let's go in.
—CALVIN AND HOBBES, BILL WATTERSON

There was once a young maiden who made a silk drum. Whoever could hear its music would have the blessing of her hand in marriage. One by one, young men came from far and wide, but not one could hear a sound.

Finally, there was but one young man left to come and listen. He sat patiently. He waited. He listened.

Then he spoke, "I can hear the music of silence."

The maiden said to him, "Then you will be my husband, for you have heard the sound of my heart."

Okay. I confess. This guy is out of my league. Given my own history and confusion in trying to understand women, if you can tell me that there is a man alive with this kind of skill, I stand in awe.

Get quiet—in order to hear silence. I'm with Calvin: this is making me nervous. Can we talk about something else?

~~~

Summer has migrated from our island, and this morning I walk the pathway of my garden, tickled to be here, probably because I feel the complete lack of urgency that comes with late autumn and early winter.

During the summer, my garden was brimming, vivid, lush, and full of energy. My activity mirrored those characteristics as I stayed busy in upkeep mode, daily working among the plants—fixing, tidying, and enhancing.

Summer garden mode is similar to how my work life proceeds most of the time, with its multitasking and nonstop activity. I've noticed, though, that if I live this way all the time, my soul shrivels. I wasn't designed to tidy up, fix, and plan 24-7.

I look at my garden now, in late autumn. Around the pathway, the plant life is a different palette: muted, soft, and tranquil. The red-twig dogwoods hold on to a few lasting leaves, now copper, deep butter, and burnished red. Around the garden perimeter, red tones take over in the crimson leaves on sumac and *Euonymus*.

A reader sent me this insight: "Perhaps, Terry, we might consider that we go within for the next growth season. As with nature, we humans need to take the time to silence ourselves from time to time in order to reflect, hear, rest, and learn."

Jazz musicians understand the importance of space between the notes in their music. And the space is intentional. In other words, this isn't passive. I choose to make space.

~~~~~~

A Powerful Pause for the Days Ahead

Where is that silent space for you?

And what, exactly, do you hear?

48

God's Other Book

My book is the nature of created things, and as often
as I have a mind to read the words of God, they are at
my hand.

—ST. ANTHONY THE GREAT

Six-year-old Johnny wanted to try out for a part in the school play. His mother knew that he'd set his heart on it, but she feared he would not be chosen. On the day the parts were assigned, Johnny, back from school, rushed into his mother's arms bursting with pride and excitement.

"Mother—guess what! I got the best part! I've been chosen to clap and cheer."

Borrowing from Barbara Brown Taylor, that which draws me to faith is not the believing parts, but the beholding parts. In other words, awe always precedes faith.

We are on the morning commuter ferry, from Vashon Island to Seattle. A snow-covered Mount Rainier dominates the panorama, looking imperial in the dawn light. (It is true. Here in the Northwest, the first time you see Mount Rainier, you do a double take. Some divine sleight of hand. Where'd that mountain come from?)

A woman stands at the window and stares. She is wide-eyed, as if she is surprised by the mountain or seeing it for the first time. All the other early-morning commuters (and there are many) go about their business: reading the newspaper, drinking coffee, paying bills, talking with friends, napping on benches.

"Look," the woman announces loudly, "we can see the mountain."

She has the demeanor of a person "not all there." You know what I mean. Clearly she embarrasses most of us, and most of us try to ignore her. We knowingly smile at one another and roll our eyes, code for, "She's not normal."

"Look," she says again, pointing this time, almost reverential, "the mountain."

I look out the window toward the place she indicates to no one in particular. The rising sun rests on the Cascade mountain ridgeline. As our ferry travels east, the shaft of light glistens and dances across the water, a pathway from the ferry to the sky. Rainier, venerable in this morning light, appears etched in pencil. The water of the Puget Sound is gunmetal gray, and calm. This scene is serene, and comforting. Above the Cascades, a blue-tinted sky. High above Rainier hangs a crescent moon. Fog lingers in Tacoma Harbor. I put down my newspaper, absorbing the pageant, and my worries recede.

A morning vista as sacrament: a dose of grace, a brew that's fortifying, settling.

"Look," the woman is talking again. "The mountain. Look everyone, the mountain."

To exit the ferry, we walk by the woman (still standing, still pointing, still talking), wondering, I suppose, what went wrong in her life, what finally snapped, and what made her leave her senses. How sad for her. We walk hurriedly, you know, in order to take care of those more important obligations awaiting us in our day. However, on this morning, the "crazy woman" is my sage—my seer, my rabbi, my priest, my pastor. She is my reminder. She *sees*, without the extra layers of defense. She sees without a need for justification, skepticism, evaluation, or any motivation to impress. "Look how beautiful," she says, "the mountain."

To see life in its mysterious and extravagant fullness begins with an inner disarmament. Sooner or later we need to remove the pieces of the armor we wear that keep us from allowing life in.

Most of the time, I prefer my armor—my resume, my title, my busyness, my distractions, my stuff. My armor keeps me safe. But it also keeps me from seeing. From feeling. From paying attention. But, hey, it's a small price to pay. At least I'm not crazy.

It is no secret that we drug ourselves. And it's all too easy to point the finger at those whose drug comes in pill or needle form. Trouble is, I have found that anger, resentment, fear, apathy, self-pity, shame, and a victim mentality are just as effective. They all serve the same purpose. Each one, numbing us, keeps wonder (ecstasy, awe, amazement, and grace) at bay.

Public opinion is a powerful thing. I think about how those of us on the ferry conspired to agree about the crazy woman. "We're sane, she's crazy," we reassured each other. Is it possible that we need numbers on our side, because deep down, we know that only crazy people can see? That the Spirit can *madden* us, and drive us, literally, out of our senses—or is it fully *into* our senses?—just like the psalm that reminds us that "They shall get drunk on the fullness of thy house."

Is that what I'm afraid of, intoxication with this life? What if we are here to get lost, to fall in love with life, to give in to the courage to be mad with the wonder of it all, to live and dance on the edge of grace, where we have nothing to show to justify our existence?

To see is to change.

Seeing allows awe.

And awe gives birth to gratitude.

Gratitude makes space for attention.

And, in the words of Simone Weil: "Absolute unmixed attention is prayer."

What did you do today? It was a good day. I clapped and cheered.

Inspirations

I perform admiration. Come with me. . . . And do the same.

—MARY OLIVER, *WINTER HOURS*

～～～～～～～～～～～～～～～～～～～～～～～～～～～

A Powerful Pause for the Days Ahead

Spend some time looking at clouds or trees or water or mountains. Practice admiration. In your own way, clap and cheer. Or stand up and shout, "Bravo!"

> ～～ **See** a mountain, even if you're not from Seattle, at www.loyolapress.com/powerofpause by clicking on Book Extras.

49

Kiss Still Works

What has been lost is the true beholding of the light from the inner eyes. Grace is given to heal that inner sight, to open our eyes again to the goodness that is deep within us, for God is within us. The grace of Christ restores us to our original simplicity.

—JOHN SCOTTUS ERIUGENA, IN *JOHN SCOTTUS ERIUGENA*, DEIRDRE CARBINE

I stand by the bed where a young woman lies, her face postoperative, her mouth twisted in palsy, clownish. A tiny twig of the facial nerve, the one to the muscles of her mouth, has been severed. The surgeon had followed with religious fervor the curve of her flesh; I promise you that. Nevertheless, to remove the tumor in her cheek, I had cut the little nerve.

Her young husband is in the room. He stands on the opposite side of the bed, and together they seem to dwell in the evening lamplight, isolated from me, private. Who are they, I ask myself, he and this wry mouth I have made, who gaze at and touch each other so generously, greedily? The young woman speaks.

"Will my mouth always be like this?" She asks.

"Yes," I say, "it will. It is because the nerve was cut."

She nods, and is silent. But the young man smiles.

"I like it," he says. "It is kind of cute."

All at once I *know* who he is. I understand, and I lower my gaze. One is not bold in an encounter with a god. Unmindful, he bends to kiss her crooked mouth, and I am so close, I can see how he twists his own lips to accommodate to hers, to show her that their kiss still works.

—RICHARD SELZER, *MORTAL LESSONS*

This past weekend I led a conference in northern Arkansas (at "the mountain," Mount Sequoyah), where I was filling in for another speaker. I inherited the topic and title: Extreme Makeover—God Edition. I need to confess my initial discomfort. Did I have the right things to say? And the word *makeover* automatically made me wonder what was missing in *my* life.

To say that makeovers are a fixation in our culture would be, well, one whopper of an understatement, since there are more anti-wrinkle creams on the market than we can count. And we spend billions of dollars per year just on those creams to help us look younger.

But it's not about the makeover, is it? It's about this cultural full-court press that we are compelled to remake ourselves into someone who will be acceptable. Lovable even, and, one would hope, successful. Because apparently whoever we are now, well, just isn't enough.

So I give in to the latest can't-miss cream or treadmill or book or seminar that promises to make me spiritually or psychologically state of the art. As if I need to add something to my life to make it okay. To see the image and goodness of God within me would be, apparently, too much to ask. At least, not until I've had my "makeover."

That was ingrained in me as a kid, where my church taught me that grace had a whole lot to do with giving up drinking and smoking and swearing and playing cards and dancing and women. Giving up dancing was easy because I wasn't any good at it. And smoking burned my throat. And drinking a whole bottle of peppermint schnapps once, on a dare, made me throw up. And women, well, they just confused me. (And yes, they still do. And any man who tells you otherwise is yanking your chain.)

Long story short, by college, I didn't drink or smoke or swear or play cards or dance or even think about women. (Okay, I'm lying about the women part. I did a lot of thinking—and thought if I was lucky I'd find at least one woman versatile in all those trespasses.) So I learned the lingo and played the part. But it had absolutely nothing to do with grace.

The game plan was simple: getting to heaven. Jesus was like some Travel Agent for Eternity. And my costume? It was window dressing. My uniform for the divine hall monitor, my free pass. Anything to keep God from being less than thrilled.

Because in the end, all I was, was afraid. And not just afraid of God or eternal damnation. I was afraid of being found out as a fake.

What I needed was the permission to simply be human. To be just Terry. I needed to know that the divine kiss of grace still works.

～～～

It is autumn cleanup time at "the mountain." Most of the grand old trees have surrendered their leaves, which now cloak every surface. This morning the sun came out and the air felt crisp with a steady and refreshing breeze. I sat on a stone wall near the driveway. Oak leaves, the color of antique pennies, twirled and cascaded, playing tag along the asphalt. I kicked a pile of them, and it made the sound of brushes on a snare drum. It is the music of my childhood, and I smile, even become a little giddy. And in the breeze I feel that kiss of acceptance, knowing that on this day, it is enough just to be.

Inspirations

Grace strikes us when we are in great pain and restlessness. It strikes us when we walk through the dark valley of a meaningless and empty life. . . . It strikes us when, year after year, the longed-for perfection of life does not appear, when the old compulsion reign within us as they have for decades, when despair destroys all joy and courage. Sometimes at that moment a wave of light breaks into our darkness. . . . If that happens to us, we experience grace.

—PAUL TILLICH, *THE SHAKING OF THE FOUNDATIONS*

~~~~~~~~~~~~~~~~~~~~~~~~~~~~

A Powerful Pause for the Days Ahead

This week, practice the simplicity prayer, sometimes called the Jesus Prayer.

"Lord, have mercy." Or "Jesus, have mercy."

50

The Farmer's Miracle Dog

There are only two ways to live your life. One is as though nothing is a miracle. The other is as though everything is a miracle.

—ALBERT EINSTEIN, ATTRIBUTED

A farmer bought a new hunting dog. On their first day of duck hunting, the farmer shoots a duck, which falls into the lake. The retriever leaps into action, walking across the lake to retrieve the duck. The farmer rubs his eyes, incredulous. "I've got to see this again," he says. Another shot, another duck plummets into the lake. Again, the dog eagerly trots across the water to fetch the duck.

The farmer is beside himself. "This is a miracle!" he shouts. Wanting to share the miracle, he runs to his neighbor's house and urges him to return to the lake.

"Watch this," he says, "and tell me if you see anything unusual." A shot, and a duck plummets. The retriever trots across the water and returns with the duck.

"Well?" the farmer asks.

"Hm," says his neighbor, scratching his chin, "I can't say that I notice anything abnormal."

He's nuts, the farmer is thinking. "Watch again. Concentrate this time." One more shot, and another duck. The retriever dutifully walks across the water to fetch it. "Ohh." The neighbor lights up with recognition. "Now I see what's different! I don't think your dog can swim."

Most of us are good at seeing only what we want to see. We do not see the dog walking on the water because we want to be right, or normal, or in the mainstream, or theologically correct, or accepted, or afraid that anything out of the ordinary will rock our boats, emotionally and otherwise.

Most of us walk around with blinders on, whether they be blinders of hatred, arrogance, prejudice, judgment, or animosity.

Our blinders prevent us from seeing everything that is there. Ready for a simple test? Check out any FedEx truck (or company logo). Got it? What do you see? I see FedEx in purple and orange. Okay. Look again. This time, pretend you cannot read. This time, you will see an arrow. Clearly, between the E and X. This is interesting, because studies done with illiterate persons show that they see the arrow first, every time.

So. How do we get these blinders off?

Some of us want to make it about willpower or effort, forcing ourselves to see what is not really there. Sort of like squinting hard to see the mother of Jesus imprinted in a cheese sandwich.

I really like the story in the Gospel of John about a blind beggar. People argued over what made him blind, and people argued over whose fault it was, and whether Jesus had the credentials to spit in the mud and make a poultice. But to the blind man it didn't matter. He simply said, "All I know is that a while ago I was blind, but now I can see."

It has something to do with letting go. When you let go, you can be grateful for what you receive. When you're grateful, you don't have to have every question settled. It's enough just to celebrate.

The farmer's secret? He saw himself as the luckiest man on earth—his dog could walk on water! He didn't need to know how that was possible—he just wanted to spread the joy.

Inspirations
We thank Thee.
For Thy miracles which are daily with us,
For Thy continual marvels.

—JEWISH PRAYER

A Powerful Pause for the Days Ahead

Walk in a garden or park (or along a river or lake, or on a prairie) and pay close attention. Look for miracles, especially in the small things.

51

Heaven on Earth

The aim of life is to live, and to live means to be aware,
joyously, drunkenly, serenely, divinely aware.

—HENRY MILLER, *TROPIC OF CAPRICORN*

This tastes like heaven," says my son, Zach, eating from a small bag of popcorn, picking out one kernel at a time.

I take a sip of coffee and close my eyes. My son is right. This does taste like heaven.

I heard a lot about heaven in the church of my youth, although, on balance, I heard a good deal more about hell. It was some calculated motivational tool to make heaven seem that much more appealing. What was clear was the objective: getting there—heaven, that is. Trouble was, I was never much drawn to the heaven portrayed in those sermons of my youth because there was no movie preview about exactly what we'd be doing when we got there. And, what's really to enjoy about people (mostly old people) in white suits sitting around playing elevator music? For a young boy, that had all the enticement of a twenty-four-hour Lawrence Welk special, with an all-accordion choir.

Predictably, I was mostly frightened of hell. Heaven was used to soothe my regrets. So I could say, "At least I'm going to heaven," if I was asked—which I was, daily. But one thing was clear; heaven had nothing to do with today or with the way I lived my life today.

In his book *Too Small to Ignore*, Wess Stafford (president of Compassion International, www.compassion.com) tells a story from his childhood on the Ivory Coast of Africa. A convoy of French colonial officials visited a village to do a government survey. They asked the village elders about their "expectations of the future." The surveyors wanted number estimates of what the elders expected in terms of the village's growth and development.

> The chief and his tribal elders tried to explain to their exasperated visitors that they really didn't know the answers to those kinds of questions, because the future had not yet arrived. When the time came to pass, then the results would be apparent. This, to be sure, made the officials less than pleased. And they left, in a huff.
>
> That day, at dusk, the village gathered in the chief's courtyard. He said, "I want to talk to the children tonight."
>
> "We are not like them," the chief said. "To them time is everything . . . the smaller that men can measure the day, the more angry they seem to be.

"The present is now—the days we live today. This is God's gift to us. It is meant to be enjoyed and lived to the fullest. They miss so much of the joy of today all around them. Did you notice that as they stormed into our village, they didn't notice it is the best of the mango season? Though we offered them peanuts, they did not even taste them. They did not hear the birds in the trees or the laughter in the marketplace. We touched them with our hands, but they did not really see us.

"They miss much of the present time, because all they care about is the unknowable, the future. . . . The present is all we can fully know and experience, so we must.

"We must love each other. We must smell the hibiscus flowers. We must hear the singing of the weaverbirds and the grunts of the lions. We must taste with joy the honey and the peanut sauce on the rice. We must laugh and cry and live."

Whether he knew it or not, the village chief took Jesus seriously. Remember when Jesus said, "Behold, the kingdom of God is in the midst of you." Meaning right now, in the midst of you—right here. Meaning this moment can be the Sacrament of the Blessed Present, this ordinary moment, a container of grace.

Meaning also that the visible and the invisible are one. The Celts called some places "thin places," places in which the sacred is almost palpable.

Elizabeth Barrett Browning wrote:

Earth's crammed with heaven,
And every common bush afire with God;
But only those who see take off their shoes.
The rest sit around it and pluck blackberries.

We can walk in reverence, taking off our shoes. Or we can tell ourselves that the kingdom is yet to be, somewhere in the future, something for which we are willing to give up today. And we give up who we are today, for who we think we should be.

I experience this jarring disconnect while watching any celebrated event on TV. Like this past Super Bowl for example. (I'll refrain from reminding you that Seattle lost, and that the officials were part of a conspiracy meant to rob us from the ecstasy of victory. But no worries, I'm over it. Really. I just will never take another speaking job in Pittsburgh—unless they pay through the nose.)

I was helped this past month by reading Eugene O'Kelly's book, *Chasing Daylight*. It's the story about the last three months of his life.

O'Kelly reinforces what we all know to be true. This moment, I have a choice. I can receive the gift of life and embrace it, and immerse myself in it. Or, continue to live in oblivion, asleep, distracted, and waiting. And in the process, we bury the very things that might set us free (borrowing from Stephen Levine). Such as stopping, stillness, listening, hearing, tasting, touching, seeing, smelling, and embracing.

In our Western mind-set, living in the present becomes a staged event. It's staged to be spiritual, as if this is something we must orchestrate. And we sit stewing in the juices of our self-consciousness. Am I present? What am I doing right or wrong? All the while, we're missing the point.

A Hasidic rabbi was interrupted by one of his followers while he was tending his garden. "What would you do, Rabbi," the student asked, "if you knew the messiah was coming today?" Stroking his beard and pursing his lips, the rabbi replied, "Well, I would continue to water my garden."

Last week I sat with friends on a beach south of Sarasota, Florida. We watched the sun set behind the stark flat-line horizon of the Gulf of Mexico. We were the only people on the beach. Just above the horizon, the orb, a perfect circle, appeared to hold, now incandescent on a slate blue screen. This scene was so vivid that it took on the appearance of a special effect. The sun was the color of embers at the bottom of a bonfire. As if on cue, porpoises scrolled through the water, not even twenty feet from shore, breaking the sun's shimmer imprinted on the water's surface.

There is nothing gained by cataloging such a moment. I need to let it be. I take my shoes off.

The other night, Zach was outside when I told him it was time for bed.

"I can't," he said.

"Why?"

"First I need to say good night to the world."

In his bones, he knew that he didn't need to wait for a better moment. He understood that heaven was right here and now.

～～～～～～～～～～

A Powerful Pause for the Days Ahead

Go barefoot sometime this week, even if you can only do that inside. Feel the earth or sand or wood or tile. Consider that you are walking on holy ground and stop to take notice of heaven.

> ～ **Read** more about thin places and become more aware of the thin places in your life. Visit www.loyolapress.com/powerofpause and click on Book Extras.

52

For Thanksgiving: Living Room

If the only prayer you said in your whole life was, "thank you," that would suffice.

—MEISTER ECKHART, ATTRIBUTED

Years ago I had the experience of sitting around in a living room with a bunch of people and singing and playing, and it was like a spiritual experience, it was wonderful," Emmylou Harris says, on the Nitty Gritty Dirt Band CD, *Will the Circle Be Unbroken*. "Over the years of making records we've all gotten a little too technical and too hung up on getting things perfect. We've lost the living room. The living room has gone out of the music. Today, we got it back."

Most of us can relate. I remember being in my first garden, on my knees in April, rooting around the soil looking for the tubers of our peonies. I saw only blank soil and was afraid something terrible happened to my new children. Gardening was new to me, and I did not know that peonies could be notoriously late in showing their conical tubers. After some minor excavating, I found what I was looking for, and I grinned and laughed to the woods and the sky, tickled at what I found, and thrilled at the magic that awaited. I remember that young gardener, who was unself-conscious. Never once did I ask the question, "Am I doing this right?" I was simply glad to be digging in the dirt. It was my living room.

We are likely to ask, "So what do we need to do, to get the living room back?" Because our Western mentality finds solace in the five steps that allow for some resolution. Sort of like the medical school administrators who found that their fifth-year students had lost the enthusiasm, warmth, and empathy that had characterized their freshman year. To fix this, the school presented a mandatory class on compassion.

Or, consider some adults watching a group of very young kids playing sandlot baseball, using discarded boxes for bases, a potpourri of equipment, and an odd formula for scoring and for choosing up teams. The air is filled with whooping and unmitigated pleasure. The adults, however, wanting to be helpful, decided to step in, in order to give the kids instruction and a clearer understanding of the rules. Then the adults wondered why some of the kids decided to quit playing because the game wasn't fun anymore.

Our good intentions for control don't necessarily benefit us. When we're so focused on the right notes, we miss the music.

I have a friend who went into his garden to pray. The fragrance undid him. He was smitten by an Asiatic lily—so intoxicating, mesmerizing. He spent the next twenty minutes giddy as a kid, he told me. "I was so undone," he lamented, "I forgot to pray."

"And I felt chastised and guilty. Until it hit me. Being undone by the lily and savoring its beauty *was* my prayer."

In that moment, my friend got back the living room.

～～～～～～～～～～～～～～～～～～～～～～～～～～～

A Powerful Pause for the Days Ahead

Sometime today, I invite you to set aside the manual, or the rules, or anything else that causes you to focus on perfection rather than on the moment.

～～ **Visit** www.loyolapress.com/powerofpause and click on Book Extras to re-take the Power of Pause assessment. Write your score here _____. Are you pausing more? What are some ways you can continue to practice the power of pause?

Acknowledgments

I'm grateful to all those who presence is felt in these pages. McCartney and Lennon got it right—we do get by "with a little help from our friends."

Thanks to Jeremy Langford, my agent. Thanks to Joe Durepos, from Loyola Press, who talked about the genesis of this book while we sipped wine and watched the settling of dusk. Thanks for the kindred spirit in Tom McGrath. Big thanks to Judine O'Shea for her production magic. I am grateful to my editor Vinita Wright for her careful eye and her affection for the right word, but mostly because she is a lover of "hammock time."

To Zach Hershey and Todd Roseman, Charlie Hedges, Bill McNabb, Rich Hurst, Roy Carlisle, Chris Eaton, Leilani Goeckner, Ron Noecker, Bret Nicholaus, Steve Connor, Melissa Tomar, Karin Kurtz, Kent Kilbourne, Ed Kilbourne, Celia Whitler, Andrea Liston, Lee Jaster and others who have read this manuscript, encouraged me, and helped make the book possible.

My list is not complete, nor can it be. There are names misplaced in the corners of my memory and names of many Sabbath Moment readers who have offered suggestions and camaraderie along the way. Know that I thank you all. And know that on my patio sits an Adirondack chair reserved for you. Whenever you're passing through, drop in; we can spend an afternoon musing as daylight grows soft and turns into stars. We can practice the power of pause.

Terry

More from Terry Hershey

Visit his personal site at www.terryhershey.com to:

- Access Terry's speaking schedule
- Subscribe to his e-newsletter
- View pictures and videos
- Browse Terry's other products
- Request a speaking engagement